Midwinter Spring

Jane W. Stevenson
June 1988
Lincoln

Midwinter Spring

Coming late to Prayer

SUSAN COUPLAND

Foreword by
Bishop Michael Ramsey

Darton Longman and Todd
London

First published in 1984 by
Darton, Longman and Todd Ltd
89 Lillie Road, London SW6 1UD

ISBN 0 232 51622 7

British Library Cataloguing in Publication Data

Coupland, Susan
  Midwinter Spring.
  1. Aged—Religious life
  I. Title
  248.8′5   BV4580

  ISBN 0–232–51622–7

Phototypeset by Input Typesetting, London SW19 8DR
Printed in Great Britain by Anchor Brendon Ltd, Tiptree, Essex

To
Ron, June and Damian,
and the 1978 Celebration Team
in gratitude and love

Contents

Foreword

This is an unusual and exciting book. It tells of the experience of prayer in one who turned to it when old and seems in so doing to become young again in her relation to God which is what prayer means. The joys and the worries, the simplicity and the manysidedness, the inner peace and the toil are told with an authenticity likely to help people of any age.

+ MICHAEL RAMSEY

Preface

This little book is a description of a septuagenarian's attempt to learn to pray in old age. The five years' adventure has not been without the ups and downs that come at any stage of life. But there is the possibility for the elderly of a quiet but steady journey into a real relationship with God. This could bring for many people a new vitality, sometimes physical and intellectual vitality, as well as new spiritual life.

A few people have given me much-appreciated encouragement. The Reverend Neville Ward has read the book and given most generous and valuable advice and criticism. Canon R. Granger, Brother Damian, s.s.f., and Miss G. Hancock have given unstinted support. Mrs June Granger has suggested many of the books included in the reading list. The fellowship of a happy and lively church has played a large part in the experiences described.

I am very grateful to Darton, Longman and Todd for launching the first published work of a septuagenarian and for the help shown by all their staff.

SUSAN COUPLAND

Acknowledgements

I am grateful to A. R. Mowbray & Co. Ltd for permission to quote from *Learning about Retreats* by Sister Joanna Baldwin and *Letters of Direction* by the Abbé de Tourville; to John Murray (Publishers) Ltd for permission to quote from 'House of Rest' in *Collected Poems* by John Betjeman; and to S.P.C.K. for permission to quote from *One Man's Prayers* by George Appleton and *Procession of Passion Prayers* by Eric Milner White.

1

The Start of an Adventure

And Abraham was seventy and five years old when he
departed out of Haran. (Genesis 12:4)

Abraham was a very old man when he began one of the
greatest adventures in the world's history. It may have been
partly an adventure of a nomadic tribe, aimed at new lands,
wealth and trade. But it was certainly also a spiritual adventure,
an adventure of faith in which Abraham seems to have had
some direct experience of God, like so many Old Testament
leaders and prophets. He was sure not only that he was talking
to God, but that God was talking to him and giving him precise
commands and instructions. He was ordered to make a great
journey from Haran into Canaan, described at that time as a
land flowing with milk and honey. In return for Abraham's
trust and obedience, God promised possession of Canaan. He
also promised that Abraham's descendants should become a
great nation and that Abraham himself would become famous.
It was difficult to trust the promise that he should become the
father of a great nation because he and his wife had no children
and Sarah was well past the age of childbearing.

But Abraham did trust his God, and the child Isaac was
born. Through the promised descendants came the first kings,
Saul and David, and then a line of prophets foretold that a
messiah should come from the house of David.

Jesus, the Messiah, was born in the greatest days of the
Roman Empire, an empire that has crumbled to dust. But as
I started this book, the lordship of the child born in Bethlehem
was being proclaimed by Pope John Paul in Wembley Stadium.

1

A great sea of joyful, holiday-making, and yet praying Catholics were responding to the Pope's great affirmation. It is an exciting new landmark in the adventure that Abraham started when he left Haran for Canaan.

Abraham's adventure was not just a geographical journey; it was an adventure of trust and faith in his God. This trust and faith are prayer.

Like Abraham, I, too, am seventy-five as I begin to write this little book. I had moved towards a relationship with God on other occasions in my life, but the ego had always been at the centre and God on the periphery of my thinking and my loving. I first knew him as a close friend with whom I could have plain speech and to whom I could open all my heart when I was seventy. So on the basis of only five years' experience, I have the presumption to start a book, and perhaps my adventure is as difficult as Abraham's was. For Abraham was faced with country of which he was ignorant, and that may be the case for me, too, only in a spiritual sense.

It is quite simply the adventure of being born again. That experience in old age is a very joyful one, but it can also bring disturbances as well as new life.

I still find it difficult to define or to explain what happened – and is still happening – with precision. One of the best accounts I have read of the changes was in a *Guardian* article of a few years ago which my vicar shoved under my nose with a chuckle at the start of a parish church council meeting. It was by Fred Milson and entitled 'Face to Faith: Glad to be Old'. Starting with the question that Nicodemus put to Jesus, 'Can a man be born again when he is old?', he sums up in his second paragraph:

> The old should be, and often are, born again. What kind of creatures will they become? Petulant, pontifical, boring, nostalgic, cynical, sentimental, egotistical, despairing, censorious? Or wise and tolerant? Granted sufficient health and means, age can be, not just an addendum, but a distinctive period. The thousands of pensioners travelling round the

country in coaches are having new experiences, getting to know the world better before they leave it.

He speaks of the heart of the experience as that of spiritual penitence. In defining the nature of penitence, he suggests that in old age, this includes looking 'with compassion on the brash, insensitive youngster he was half a century ago'.

And that was included in my penitence. But when people in the town looked at me around the age of seventy and said, 'You look so well and happy, what has happened to you?' I was too much of a coward to answer, 'I'm searching for God, and the search gives me joy.'

This book will be concerned mainly with that search, with the spiritual adventure of a very ordinary woman between the age of seventy and seventy-five and with her hope that there will be others who will want to share with her the new life and joy that can be experienced at any stage of life.

But no spiritual journey starts at seventy or at any other age, though there may be a new and distinctive phase. From day to day we become more and more the people we have always been. The post-repentance period is not comprehensible for me without a clear look at the 'brash insensitive youngster' and, in my own case, at the over-burdened woman I was for the greater part of my life.

I think it is true to say that for most of my life I was over efficient, over conscientious, and that I never had time or energy to experience the joy of God.

I was the eldest girl of a very poor working-class family – a miner's family in the North Midlands. Mother was for most of her life a semi-invalid and my father more prepared than any man I ever knew to sacrifice himself in order to give his children a sound education. We were Methodists, and in my earliest childhood I loved the vigorous hymn singing and the dramatic hour-long sermons often preached by coal miners. In my adolescence I was an effective local preacher, which meant not just preaching a sermon on Sunday but sometimes taking two or three full services at village chapels. I was in demand. I

3

enjoyed being able to make people listen to me and the business of making a service flow and integrate, and above all of preaching a sermon. I feel now that I knew very little indeed about God, and I certainly did not seek to do anything in that overworked phrase 'to the glory of God'. But people came, the congregations were good; they listened and usually approved and I enjoyed the approval. Who doesn't?

I got a kick out of showing what I could do; my command of words and a strong voice made it comparatively easy. I liked praise and approval because there was much in my life that made me feel inferior.

When, at nineteen years old, I was in danger of losing my college scholarships because my work was not of a sufficiently high standard, my father insisted, and rightly so, that I should give up all the chapel work. I knew that college and a good degree were my only hope of a richer life than most of my contemporaries enjoyed. So I pushed the chapel out of my life, and for nearly half a century I pushed God out of it, too.

When I started work, the normal springs of vitality and hope were suppressed by the effects of the Depression years, which meant periods of unemployment alternating with work in Dickensian boarding schools. The war years brought me work in a first-class grammar school, but illness on the staff and my responsibility for a large school canteen meant that sometimes I did the work of three people. Heavy Merseyside bombing and the habit of sleeplessness that sprang from it, together with the hours of teaching in damp, cold trenches, sapped the fulfilment I should have known in a very good school with an inspired headmistress. Then in 1946 family illnesses and problems began which lasted until I retired, with one very short interval. I took an immense pride in gritting my teeth, in not letting anybody down, in being an efficient realist with my feet firmly on the ground who often enjoyed herself in giving 'ineffective Christians' what I called 'a piece of my north-country mind'.

Added to this I developed a ridiculous generosity, helping all kinds of people with their problems and giving thousands of hours of free coaching to girls who needed help to win a university place. I was determined to be among the atheist sheep and not among the Christian goats. This foolish attitude is still something of a millstone around my neck.

God began to knock at my door during a five-year period of freedom, after my mother died, from 1950 to 1955. I found two great friends during this period and one of the characteristics of my encounter with God is that human affection and a desire to love God have marched together. The first friend was a middle-aged Anglican curate, John Slack, who had his roots in the Methodist ministry. People in this neighbourhood still remember him as one of the keenest theological minds and perhaps the best preacher they have ever known. He let me loose in a remarkable theological library. During the eighteen months I was able to borrow his books, I read avidly and without any system, Tillich, Maritain, Büber, Kierkegaard, Simone Weil, Von Hügel, d'Arcy, Nygren, the anonymous *Cloud of Unknowing*, William Temple, Jung, Dorothy Sayers, Calvin, Hooker, C. S. Lewis. I remember little of what I read and certainly did not become in any sense a theological student. The family clouds descended again before I had time to digest it. Yet I had read enough for theology to become for me 'a natural pasture'. For this, I shall always be very grateful to John Slack. In his long explanatory answers to my questions, John patiently laid the foundations of Christian theology for me. But there was not enough time to grow into Christian love or to discover much about the life of prayer for myself.

My other friend was a woman colleague on the staff of Petersfield High School where we were working. In her own disciplines she had a mind equal to John's. One day as I was flicking over the pages of a new copy of *Theology* in her company, I found an article by Hugh Blenkin on Charles Williams and the Way of Affirmation. I had never heard of Charles Williams before, but almost every sentence in Hugh Blenkin's article rang bells for me. For the next few months Jean and I read every book by Charles Williams that we could lay our hands on.

I knew real spiritual delight as I read *He Came Down From Heaven* with its great doctrine of co-inherence and his affirmations about the nature of love. Vaguely, I had always approved these positive ideas and criticized the Church for its failure to affirm the glory of the body and the wonder of the love between man and woman. Charles Williams related them firmly to the first article of the Creed in words of precision and beauty. The doctrine of co-inherence prepared the way for the joy I knew later when I came into a lovely company of Christian people in St Peter's, Petersfield. The doctrine of substitution became an unspoken foundation of the friendship between Jean and myself.

At this time, too, Jean introduced me to the poetry of George Herbert. In my seventies, George Herbert has become one of my guides in learning how to make conversation with God. In 1955, three of us on the school staff organized a holiday-cum-conference about Charles Williams at Milland in Hampshire. There were about sixty of us. It was an unorthodox and carefree time for most of us, with a fair dose of demanding intellectual thought and discussion. Dorothy Sayers herself lectured on Charles Williams' interpretation of Dante; she was then nearing the completion of her great translation. But it is only now in my seventies that I can begin to understand the wonderful introduction that she wrote for her work. At the time of the conference I was still showing off what I could achieve. There was a complicated ego at the centre of my life. I still had to learn the simplicity and the depth of the love that God was waiting to offer me. He was still far away on the circumference of my spiritual life.

Once again, the clouds descended. There was a decade of very heavy demands both in the family circle and at work, as a result of the closure of Petersfield High School. There was no time at all for reading of my choice and my physical energies at last began to wane.

These were uncomfortable and unhappy years in which I was fighting against myself and being a negative opponent of a Church that, secretly, I wanted to love. That became clear when ill-health forced me into early retirement and I wrote my first book. Few people expected me to live to my seventies. I decided to give my last few years to fulfilling a promise to weave stories about Petersfield, told to former pupils, into a book and print it. One of the central themes of the book was the building of St Peter's Church in Norman times.

I was startled into new life by the torrent of letters that came appreciating the story and my effort to write it at an advanced age!

For me it was a story about my heroine. But for most people it was a story about St Peter's Church, and they liked it.

In a very diffident, cowardly fashion I began to go to St Peter's Church at festivals. People knew my book but they did not know me, and they did not notice me or speak. It was a lonely business and we make sure that it does not happen now.

In 1978, when I was seventy, St Peter's held a Celebration Fortnight. Franciscan friars were to lead a mission to 'awaken' the Church and the town to the good things that Christians had to offer, and to celebrate.

I suddenly decided to hold my own small celebration to show what someone outside the Church could do! I invited some church members and drama-society friends to come to a Sunday lunch followed by a reading of Charles Williams' 'Thomas Cranmer'. The leader of the mission, Brother Damian, arrived when the lunch was nearly over. He surveyed the lunch table, pointed to an untouched sherry trifle, thick with cream, and said, 'Can I have it?' Somewhat startled, I moved to serve him a helping but he repeated, 'No, can I have it? Can you wrap it up for me? I can use it in my service tonight.'

I had not the faintest intention of going to a popular evening service where I was sure they would sing choruses and wave their arms about and sway in rhythm. But I had to see what would happen to my trifle.

The service certainly was a turning point for me, but not a startling one nor one highly charged with emotion. There was no Damascus Road experience. I was greeted with charm and courtesy by the Vicar, Brother Damian and other Franciscans, and church members.

The service was lively, efficient, jolly. It had a message and it flowed smoothly. The children gave full attention to what they were offering but were also spontaneous. I knew the kind of expertise and care needed to make those things happen together.

Late in the service, my trifle was placed in the hands of an attractive little nun, whose arms were stiffly bound in heavy splints by Brother Damian. The audience was amused, curious, attentive.

Sister Gina was given an enormous ladle spoon. She could feed the children at her feet whose tongues were hanging out, but she could not bend her arms to feed herself. The amusement mounted in the audience and then, very quietly, Damian slid a large wooden cross behind Sister Gina who, with arms outstretched along the cross beams, formed the centre point of Damian's few effective sentences about the Christ who fed the world through his helpless sufferings. I whispered under my breath, 'Charles Williams', and in a very simple way knew that I had come home. We sang a doggerel hymn which, a week before, I would have despised, but which became both my battle song and my retreat song in defeat. It contains the stanza:

> It seeks out our anger,
> Uncovers our fears,
> And gently forgives us
> The unfruitful years.

My first step into a new love of God was made very quietly in that school hall. This book is about the ups and downs of a spiritual journey of only five years since that night. But there is no doubt at all for me about the truth of the *Guardian* article quoted earlier. It is possible to be born again, to know new life, new vitality, profound joy. This is the truth I want to share with my readers, but I shall also be quite honest about the 'downs' as well as the 'ups'.

It was the courtesy of the people I met that evening which

made a deep impression on me. Saying the words, 'The grace of our Lord Jesus Christ,' often makes me remember the grace which those people reflected. The charm was not assumed, the courtesy was no formal courtesy, the hand on the shoulder was gentle. Its touch said, 'Nobody is going to push you around.' The listening was interested, the speech was genuine. These people were firm Christians, and if the grace that I was enjoying came from their God, then I wanted to know their God and I wanted to know them.

At first I wanted to be a part of them in an ordinary human way rather than in a religious sense. Seventy is a late age at which to make new friends. Perhaps one must accept that such late friendships are seldom quite the same as the long-term friendships that have helped us through the changes and chances of a working life.

I spent a week learning all I could from the Franciscans and enjoying what I learned. After they had gone, life seemed empty and I questioned, 'What next?' An encouraging card from Damian with the minutest kiss after his name gave me the impetus to write an appreciative account of the Fortnight and to start going regularly to Church. Foolish things like kisses and trifles and the nonsense and laughter that can flow in our church community, and even wicked ribaldry at times, took the solemnity and stuffiness out of what people call conversion and made my coming into the new church family very easy.

Nevertheless I wanted the real thing, and I wanted it badly. I used to look at some of the people in the church from whom goodness and sincerity flowed like a living stream and say to myself, 'I want what makes you tick'.

I felt that the all-important thing was to learn to pray, both in church with the new family and also at home in my own way. Perhaps I had read too many theology books and too many books about prayer, or perhaps I just had a foolish sense of guilt, for I was very confused about how to start. People talked knowingly about preparation, confession, meditation, contemplation, dry periods, and intercession. It all meant virtually nothing, and I thought wearily, 'What a lot of words ending in "ion".' I desperately wanted to know, to feel at the heart of myself the love of this God who had begun to come into my life. In the Teaching Week which later followed the Celebration Fortnight nobody seemed able to understand my need or to meet it. I wanted some simple five-finger exercises, and I felt resentful against people who had been praying all their lives but could not say something practical to help me. I suppose they thought of me as an intellectual who was well equipped to solve her own problems.

So that forced me to talk despairingly to Our Lord out of anger. I know now that it was a good way to begin. For despair and anger destroy all pious nonsense. I said, 'All right, Lord, I will say "Thank you" for a month, because that's how the babies start. They sing, "Thank you for the world so sweet." That's how I'll start.' And I did. I found that a month wasn't nearly long enough for the tale of my blessings and happiness, but I moved into a mood of gratitude and contentment that I wanted to share with my new church friends. That led to plans for a Thanksgiving Day in church and an effort to involve the local schools as a part of it. That, in its turn, led to some fierce opposition and criticism, for my new-fangled notions upset people and the idea of being joyful in Lent turned tradition upside down.

So, once again, I had to turn to our Lord in tears and loneliness. I just prayed without ceasing that the day would not be a total fiasco. In the event it was one of the most glorious days of my life. After weeks of rain, a midsummer sun shone in March. The church was a riot of colour and splendour, and long before 'doors opening' time children and parents poured in and a jolly puppet show telling the story of Zacchaeus set the tone for a day in which people accepted and enjoyed the opportunities for fun and worship. Prayer, for me, had 'worked' and I had begun to learn to trust the Lord I wanted to know as a friend.

But we have to accept that learning to pray in later life is a different thing from learning early in life. I have the impression that Christians who have enjoyed long years of Church membership learn the lessons of prayer in a gradual, natural way, almost imperceptibly integrating a lifetime of experiences into their prayers. But after we retire, time is short in which to learn the greatest thing in life – to search for God and to try to know him and to love him. Many great saints who have given up a whole lifetime to prayer, have said that even after fifty years they were still beginners in prayer. But that need not deter us, even though we are well on into our seventies or eighties. The parable of the latecomers to the vineyard (Matthew 20:1–16) is a plain answer to any question we may raise.

God most certainly wants us in his vineyard but I am sure it is important not to overstrain by trying to make up for lost time. Learning to pray and to love God is not something we can hurry; we must be prepared to be patient and to make haste slowly. Nor must we be discouraged by the saintly certainty of many books about prayer, often written by people in religious communities who have given much time to prayer. We must go to God in the way he points out for us as very ordinary people. Though we may have neglected him and disappointed him in the past, be very sure that he will not disappoint us now if we really trust him.

Even in five years we can know something of our land flowing with milk and honey if we so choose: even in five minutes we can throw ourselves into the arms of God's love and accept his forgiveness for the years in which we have failed to seek him.

But at this early stage there is no need to let a sense of guilt about the past oppress us. At the start of the adventure, let us begin, as Abraham did, seeking for relationship and trust. God is taking the initiative. He will do much for us each time we try to pray.

God has been looking out for us, like the father in the story of the prodigal son (Luke 15:11–32). Not only when we try to pray, but whenever we have a worry or a fear, it is a good thing to imagine the father running out to meet the son and holding him in his compassionate love. No words are necessary to start with. Let us feel the arms of a loving father round us

11

and try to give him the simple love and trust of a child who runs up to his father to give him a hug and a kiss.

That may be difficult if we have unhappy memories of our childhood father. In our young days fathers could be stern disciplinarians and sometimes there were a lot of moral platitudes about being cruel to be kind. In poor homes life could be harsh, and some of us knew more of a father's harshness than of his love. If that is so, we must try to think of another human countenance that reflects the compassionate side of a father's nature. This is easy for me at the moment, for I am writing at the time of Pope John Paul II's visit to Britain, and every time I switch on the television, there is his loving face, his arms held wide in welcome, his countenance alive with spontaneous compassion for the aged, the young and the disabled. It is not difficult to think of God as a Being, loving and compassionate like John Paul but infinitely, infinitely more so.

People wanted to tell the Pope about their gratitude for his coming and of their love for him. We, too, shall want from the start to speak to God in words and phrases. Let us not strain over words or try to find suitable phrases. Let us be very simple indeed. We could begin with two very familiar phrases: 'Our Father' and 'Just as I am'.

'Our Father.' The two simple words with which Jesus began a prayer when the disciples asked him to show them how to pray. He is a Father we can approach in confidence and trust, a Father to whom we can speak unreservedly about everything, a Father to whom we can give all our hidden or suppressed powers of love.

I suppose all of us have been in love at some time or other and most of us have married. It is quite common for lovers to whisper the name of the loved one to themselves hundreds of times a day when they first fall in love. This is the way to say 'Our Father' for the first few days, with joy, with longing and with love, quietly, happily, over and over again. All through my five years' journey I have done this. These two words can be said quietly under the breath, anywhere, any time, and they make a prayer that is perfect and whole.

I suggest it is a good thing to be content with very few words for the first few weeks, either with short phrases of this kind or with simple expressions of 'Thank you'. There should be no strain or hurry. If sleep is difficult, we can whisper, 'Our Father,' or 'My Father,' or 'Abba Father,' in a slow rhythm, and let the rhythm grow slower and slower until tiredness stops us. If we feel that our love and trust are thin on the ground, let us not be disturbed or anxious, for, as we go on quietly praying, God's Holy Spirit will join us and help us more than we can imagine at the start.

Now the second phrase, 'Just as I am'. They are the first words of a Victorian devotional hymn but there is no need at the moment to look the hymn up unless you specially want to do so. Those of us who are housewives, often use them when a friend calls without warning. We may be having a baking day or be in the middle of the Monday wash and we say, 'You must take me just as I am.' And how relieved we are if the visitor will do just that and not mind the chaos but start talking about something important to both of us while perhaps lending a hand or sharing a cup of coffee.

This is how we can ask God to come to us. Just as I am. There is no need for any special place or posture, no need to try to collect holy thoughts that do not come naturally, no need to cover up the darkness in our lives, the misery that we make for ourselves and that others make for us. He knows it all and he understands. Any attempt to seem other than we truly are will only cause strain and prevent a happy relationship. It is no good saying we are sorry about something if it is not truly the case. If we hate somebody or feel a great bitterness, it must be accepted, at least for the time being. God knows us through and through and we cannot deceive him. He still loves us.

Just as I am. We may be appalled if we take a long honest look at ourselves. But let us not be too concerned with sin and past mistakes. We shall think about them in chapter 5. Let us remember with joy that God made us and gave us all we have and above all that he is ready to give us himself. We all have some real goodness, and it is not humility to pretend otherwise for that goodness is God's gift. We have many blessings, and deep within us is an instinctive longing for wholeness of life. With the help of God's Holy Spirit we shall find this wholeness through prayer.

So at some time early in our adventure let us find ten minutes or so to sit in a quiet place and say 'Thank you' for some of the joys and blessings that are ours. To start with a 'Thank you' on a simple, practical level will often lead us on to other kinds of prayer.

This is a rather long-winded prayer I wrote during the first few weeks of my adventure: 'Dear heavenly Father, I thank you for the gift of life, for the sleep of the past night and for this morning's health and strength. I thank you, too, for the times when I have been ill because those times have taught me to appreciate health and to grow some patience and under-standing. With all my heart, I thank you for the beautiful Hampshire countryside that I can see from my window, for the freshness of this spring morning, for the sun and the wind. I love my shabby little house and I am grateful for the gifts that have helped me to earn it. Thank you for these, dear Lord, and for the work I enjoyed in the past. Above all thank you for the loving friends who come here to share fun and meals and also problems and sorrow. Thank you for the personal pleasures I enjoy here, for strong tea, hot and sweet, for hot baths, a good bed and a coal fire and for the tea and toast by the fire in the winter. Thank you for all the creative joy you have given me in cooking and writing and teaching and for all the times when your Holy Spirit has helped me in these activi-ties. Give me humility to know that all these joys are gifts from you, dear Father, and help me to grow in loving dependence on your truth and your strength.'

Many would say that is prayer on a childish and pietistic level. But I was a beginner. Such simple prayers of gratitude can lead us on to adoration of God as Creator or to make prayers for those who do not enjoy our own blessings. Sometimes all that follows is a grateful silence in which I can listen for God to speak.

Older people with a lifetime of experience behind them can also make good use of the prayers of saintly Christians who were more adult in the life of prayer than we ourselves. Such prayers can become very much our own. Here is a prayer by Cardinal Newman which combines gratitude for the past with a prayer that he may remain faithful in his old age to the covenant between God and himself.

O, my God, my whole life has been a course of mercies and blessings shown to one who has been most unworthy of them. Year after year Thou has carried me on, removed dangers from my path, refreshed me, borne with me, directed me and maintained me. And Thou never wilt forsake me, I may securely repose on Thee. While I am true to Thee, Thou wilt be superabundantly good to me. I may rest upon Thy arm, I may go to sleep on Thy bosom. Only give me and increase in me, that true loyalty to Thee, which is the bond of the covenant between Thee and me, and the pledge in my own conscience, that Thou, the supreme Good wilt not forsake me.

Nothing can really replace the movement and the yearning of our own hearts towards God, but the prayers of others can move us to that yearning and to devotion. They can be helpful when, because of old age or perhaps of overstrain, both heart and mind are very tired. It is perhaps best to sit quietly after reading such a prayer and to let one or two phrases come of their own accord to the front of the mind. If it is evening we could take this thought to bed with us, 'I may rest upon Thy arm, I may go to sleep on Thy bosom.' During the daytime, we might concentrate on the phrase, 'Loyalty to Thee which is the bond of the convenant between Thee and me'.

Many schools of prayer train people to carry a short thought or phrase with them throughout the day and to let it fill their whole being, almost unconsciously as they walk about or do routine tasks or when they are still. Such a short phrase is called a mantra. As a beginner, I have found this practice especially helpful and often use lines of hymns or short phrases from the Psalms, as for example, 'Lead me in thy truth and teach me', or 'His mercy endureth for ever'. We must all discover our own methods and phrases and the thoughts that suit us best. If we really want to pray, there may be a little difficulty at the start, but it will not take long to find out what suits our needs and to find new ways from time to time so that we are not chained by routine. It is the desire and the will that are important. The next few chapters will deal with ways of encouraging the will to prayer.

Above all we should not strain over methods or attempt long periods of prayer until we do really want to come to God through Jesus Christ. At all times we should be ready to accept a spontaneous prompting to pray or any unorthodox thought that may lead to prayer.

'To come to God through Jesus Christ.' We have to try to know God in every aspect of our lives for he is in everything, but above all we must try to know him through his Son, Jesus Christ. We must try to know him as the disciples knew him even though this is not fully possible and we must try to trust him as they did. Almost certainly, we shall betray him as they did and pick ourselves up and try again to love him and to serve him as they did. Then, as time goes on, we shall seek to make him the ground of our being.

This demands reading about him and listening to what others have to say about their life in him. In time we shall want to offer our whole life to him so that he may fill it with his presence. We can find him in the reading of the gospels, in the lives of others, in their need of us and our need of them, and in the life and work of the Church. The many ways in which the Church can help us will form a part of succeeding chapters.

In old age, the beauty of the world and the beauty of character in other people often move us much more strongly than earlier in life. Through this kind of beauty, divine beauty can be glimpsed. Simone Weil says, 'The beauty of the world is

Christ's tender smile for us coming through matter'.[1] We are all terribly aware of the ugliness, hate and evil in the world today, but beauty is also there if we keep our eyes open. It is a good thing to give thanks at the end of each day for whatever beauty there has been in our lives on that particular day. Then we can offer a prayer that we ourselves may help to preserve it and that there may always be men of good will trying, in the same way, to preserve and cherish the good things that God gives to us. In this way, older people can unconsciously build up a massive bank balance of prayer on the side of goodness, beauty and love.

Helen Keller, in her blindness and deafness could say, 'I believe that God is in me as the sun is in the colour and fragrance of a flower, the light in my darkness, the voice in my silence.' As we grow older and perhaps less able to see and to hear, perhaps also to move, let us think upon Helen Keller's sharing of God with those so much more fortunate than herself. Even if we are bedridden and very dependent upon others, our reaching out to those who serve us, our acceptance of their compassion, and our giving of gratitude and compassion in words and looks will be a form of prayer. Julian of Norwich wrote, 'I saw that all compassion in one's fellow Christians, exercised in love, is a mark of Christ's indwelling.'[2]

Let us make a final prayer to conclude this first small step in our adventure. It was made and is used in a church in central London.

Come, Holy Spirit of God, restore the lives which without you are dead. Kindle the hearts which, without you, are cold and dull. Enlighten the minds which without you are dark and blind. Fill the Church which without you is an empty shrine. And lead us Lord to pray.

1. Simone Weil, *Waiting on God*. Routledge and Kegan Paul 1952.
2. *Enfolded in Love* (Daily Readings with Julian of Norwich). Darton Longman and Todd 1980.

2

Companions in the Adventure

Abraham's contract with God could have been the result of a period of solitary prayer or 'conversation with God'. But he undertook his journey with Sarah, his wife, and with Lot, his nephew. Clearly there were such considerable herds and flocks and so many herdsmen that the land could not at one time support them. Abraham was not alone. He must have had to share with others at least a partial knowledge of his vision and his plans. The fact that others were involved in a practical sense in his adventure must have helped to keep him faithful to his decision and to his contract.

It could be this way for us, too. Much of our conversation will be with God in private. The new relationship will be primarily between God and me. But if we can have companions for the adventure, and sometimes share our joy and our difficulties in praying, the journey will be enriched and we shall give and take the blessings that come with any genuine new relationship.

For many married people, however, a problem may arise early in the adventure. One partner may want very much to learn to pray but the other does not receive the impulse. In old age the marriage partnership has probably shaken down to good-humoured tolerance of what each regards as the other's foibles. It is usually the woman who turns first to prayer, and many a time in my childhood I heard practical working class men say with tolerant contempt, 'Oh, the missus is a bit daft-like just now, she's got religion.' Well, it may not be so daft-like of the woman to take to religion in retirement. The husband has given up the day-to-day grind and really does retire. His wife still has to plod on with the eternal housework and provision of meals. If she takes to something that gives her a new life, new interests, new companions, a new dynamo in her existence, who shall blame her? She has probably had little time hitherto for the kind of hobbies which her husband enjoys.

Women usually have a stronger family sense, and once their own children have grown up and married, there is time to consider the growing family, to understand its problems and to be worried about individual members. Prayer is a way in which such women can open their hearts about their often necessarily hidden concern, can share their worries, and try to understand God's care for their loved ones.

A wife will usually want her husband to share her desire to pray, but on his side there may be indifference, reluctance or even opposition, especially if she gives the impression of being too devout. Men do seem to be less religious in the traditional sense than women. They easily become resentful about their wives going out to church and leaving them alone at home. They may begin to wonder if the church is coming first with their wives. It is hard to judge in this matter. But if a wife's devotion is too pietistic and obvious, her husband can be deeply hurt and at the same time not know how to express his hurt.

In recent months three wives from three different parishes have talked to me about this problem. I find this surprising since I am unmarried and without any training in counselling or any special character traits. I said to one of them, 'Why do you come to me? How can I possibly understand your marriage problems?' She answered, 'You aren't a clergyman and you aren't a counsellor. You are just an ordinary, homely woman, and so it's easy to talk to you and to tell you that I want the freedom *you* have, to worship as I like and when I like. You can do this and so you'll understand what I want.'

I replied, 'And you are just an ordinary, homely woman and it's easy to tell you that I would give a very great deal in my old age to have the comfort and support of a husband like yours, interesting, creative, kind, reliable. I would be prepared to give up nearly all my church practices and involvements to have a husband like yours.' She was very shaken. Women sometimes fail to understand that love of God as Creator can be expressed in so many other ways than through prayer and church worship. A man who creates a lovely garden, writes or paints or makes music, who works over a long period to make his children a swimming pool, who just loves and cherishes his wife and family, is acting in a way that reflects the faithful, creative love of God. But I think it is an excellent thing if both husband and wife can come together with a tolerant priest or counsellor – or perhaps just an ordinary, homely old man or woman – and work out some practical conclusions about how each can have some time for his or her own interests and still maintain the love and cherishing promised in their marriage vows.

The state of health of elderly people reading this little book may be a determining factor in the matter of companionship in the life of prayer. Some old people go on being active well on into their nineties, able to go to a church, to find friends there, and to pray with fellow Christians. But some may be house-bound or bedridden, enjoying only occasional contact with other people who pray. It is important to think carefully about how they can be helped and how they can help themselves.

Let us consider the active group first. It could be some little time after we have started to pray in private that the urge will come to go to church ourselves. But for many people it will certainly come. I am sure that the prompting should be accepted. If we are to pray as our Lord taught us to pray, we must move away from the early concentration on our own needs, to prayer for other people. The church will help us greatly to pray for others, not only for those in the congreg-ation, but for those with special needs in all parts of the world. As we pray, 'Thy Kingdom come,' we shall begin to understand that the Kingdom is not just for us and our immediate circle but for Christians everywhere.

To develop the imagination, the understanding, and the power to pray for people we shall never see, will be a test of the generosity of our prayer. The church will help us to find a way. And if you are fortunate enough to find a church like mine, you will be enormously helped by the sheer weight of love, happiness and understanding that is present in a strong church. There is also the deep kindness and forgiveness when one fails and makes mistakes. All these qualities draw us quietly, imperceptibly, to God, and to an understanding of his love so that we want to pray for people we may never see and who need so badly the blessings that are poured out on us.

Church-going may not always be so easy. We are told quite plainly in one of the two great commandments that it is a duty to love our neighbour and that means the people sitting around us in church. This may be much more difficult in your church than in mine. But always, throughout life, we have to meet and to live with many different types of people. There are the lovable and the likable to whom we turn easily, and there are the maddeningly infuriating know-alls we just can't stand, the breezy and the taciturn and those who like the sound of their own voices. There are those who always go the extra mile and those who let us down. It is not a bad exercise to consider these categories and to realize that some people would have to put us, too, into one or other of them.

The church will help us, especially if we go to a church where a communion service or Eucharist is a central part of the life of the church. The lovely word 'Eucharist' means 'Thanks-giving'. We cannot offer thanks for the promises of Jesus at the Last Supper, unless we make an honest attempt to forgive those who hurt or irritate us. And in the same way others will have to extend the same forgiveness to us. We cannot say, 'We are one body because we all share one bread,' in sincerity unless we turn our hearts towards Jesus on the cross and his forgiving love.

I sometimes find this very difficult. So here is a prayer about it. It is clumsily expressed and not so neat or beautiful as the Collect which will follow it. But I think it is a good thing sometimes to write down our prayers however imperfect they may be.

Dear Lord Jesus Christ, who commanded us to love our neighbours as ourselves, make me much more wide awake to the needs and hopes and loves of those I meet from day to day. Give me a share in your love and understanding, the love that enabled you to pierce the defences of the outer man and to understand the longing that is deep in everyone's heart. And give me the courage to speak your truth and love with my neighbour.

Here is the Collect, neat and lovely:

> Almighty God,
> You have taught us through your son,
> That love is the fulfilling of the law,
> Grant that we may love you with our whole heart
> and our neighbours as ourselves,
> Through Jesus Christ, Our Lord. Amen.

Having made a decision to join a church, the question may arise, 'Which Church?' if there is a choice.

For many the choice will be according to denomination. In sparsely populated areas, the Church of England may be the only church available. It may appeal because of the links between Church and State, because of its parish organization, and because the Parish Eucharist is one that seems to meet the spiritual needs of large numbers of people. The Roman Catholic Church has more unity and authority than the other churches. The Mass has a strong appeal for those who love music and formal worship.

In the Methodist, Baptist and United Reformed Churches, lay people usually play a larger part than in the episcopal churches. They appoint ministers, conduct services, and preach sermons. In the Salvation Army and in the new house churches which are increasing on the housing estates, the services can be very informal. Much depends on whether an elderly person still has the energy and inclination to examine the different churches and choose.

If there is no leaning towards a special denomination perhaps the best way for an older person to choose is on two counts. I suggest it would be wise to choose a church as near to one's home as possible and, secondly, to choose one where both the services and the social life are vital and warm. It is an enormous help if there is a priest or minister who is outgoing, tolerant and kindly, a man who knows how to listen to his flock and to organize a caring ministry among his people. But, of course, it may take some time to evaluate these qualities. A social life that is lively can give us rich relationships with other Christians, and the growth of happy, human relationship will, in turn, help our relationship with God and our devotional life.

A newcomer to a church in old age will almost certainly feel that he is the lonely one, the odd man out. But that will soon pass; there will be plenty of lonely people already in the church. Don't begin an obtrusive search for them, but be ready, if they cross your path, to give to, as well as to take from, the new family. There will be people much younger than ourselves with heartaches and problems and some with incurable illnesses. Have mind and heart ready to respond to people in any way whatever and the strangeness will soon pass. If you have practical gifts and can help with coffee mornings or cleaning, with visiting or repair jobs, with care of church linen or vestments, or if you have artistic or musical gifts, let these be known. Any lively church will find a niche for gifts and services and you will soon be praying for people who need you just as much as you need them. You will become a part of a praying family and will discover the joy of belonging to a Christian community.

For me there is one Anglican service which meets my needs very fully. This is the Eucharist or Parish Communion. I do not know the Roman Catholic Mass well nor the Methodist Holy Communion or Lord's Supper, but I know that all the services are very similar in structure and that the words are often nearly identical. There is a depth and richness in this service which almost always helps me to draw near to God and gathers up the experiences and the prayer of the days preceding the service.

Neville Ward expresses how I feel about this service: 'Human beings cannot live by the immediately useful alone. They need the sacramental, they need life's depth and the depth in themselves signified and addressed.'[1]

There are many links between the Eucharist and my own private prayer. Some can be expressed but for some there are no words. There is a mystery of love in this service which is inexpressible and this is probably the most precious thing of all. But I cannot write about it.

Preparation for the Eucharist often fills my prayer time on Saturday evening. It is often possible to carry some thought from the lessons or the Collect to bed and then to resume it on Sunday morning and to hold on to it in church. For instance, on the first Sunday in the Church's year, Advent Sunday, it might be, 'Your son, Jesus Christ, came to us in great humility.' If I have not done the preparatory reading, there are a number of short phrases or lines from hymns on which I might centre my thought. One is the first line of a lovely hymn, 'Come down, O Love Divine', and often as I kneel to pray, I begin with

> Jesus, my Lord, I Thee adore,
> O, make me love Thee more and more.

These two lines are very simple but they sum up the purpose of the Eucharist and my relationship with my Lord.

Among the hymns that we sing in church or hear on the radio or television, it is a good thing to keep alert for those that specially appeal to us, and those which we can memorize easily. There will be times in old age when we shall be too tired or ill to pray actively, when we can rest ourselves in the arms of the Good Shepherd and think quietly of some of these phrases that we have shared in the Eucharist. One of my favourites at the moment is an old-fashioned Methodist hymn, 'O, for a heart to praise my God', and another, 'O Thou not made with hands', which suggests the humble and cheerfully ordinary ways in which we can all play a part in building 'God's own Jerusalem'.

1. Neville Ward, *Beyond Tomorrow.* Epworth Press 1981.

Thou art where'er the proud
In humbleness melts down;
Where self itself yields up;
Where martyrs win their crown;
Where faithful souls possess
Themselves in perfect peace.

Where in life's common ways
With cheerful feet we go;
Where in His steps we tread
Who trod the way of woe;
Where He is in the heart,
City of God, Thou art.

There is, too, a lovely evening hymn, 'The sun is sinking fast, the daylight dies', in which we can fold up our wills into the Being of Our Lord as we think deeply about his sacrifice.

In our church, during the ten minutes before the service, there is a babble of conversation. Some may think this is wrong and would prefer a silence. We are all different personalities and do well to accept our differences. I, however, like this cheerful start. We may see some people only once a week and it is an opportunity to get news of friends, of those abroad or in hospital, of the new home or the new car and of the children's prospects at school. For the old, this may save the expense of a letter or a phone call. If we learn of a distress, we can hold the friend who suffers up to our Lord during the time of prayer in the Eucharist. For these are our companions in the journey to God and the hour that follows is for many of us the most important hour in the whole week. My friends help to carry my burdens, and I hope that I, too, help to carry theirs, and together we turn to the Love that cares about everything that happens to us.

The new friends I began to make after Celebration Fortnight clearly had their lives centred on God and, if I was to know their friendship, I decided that my life would have to be centred on God, too. Human love and God's love have, in the past five years been inextricably interwoven, and so I come, step by step, nearer to God through the goodness of my friends to me. They reflect the nature of a God who is a loving Father, of a Jesus who is a Friend and a Brother. The inner circle of people I can count on the fingers of my hands but there must be at least fifty more with whom I have shared my home and often my doubts, thoughts and joys. A wonderful feast of happiness and friendship. With such friendship, one hardly needs to learn how to pray. Prayer is at the heart of the love offered to me, and responded to by me.

This affection and the peace of God which is interwoven with it are at the heart of a new life in old age which has been physical as well as spiritual, intellectual as well as devotional.

Our Anglican Eucharist is a service that includes all I need in my relationship with God and is a power house for my own prayer during the week. It is, first of all, a time of thankfulness and of offering, of offering of our whole selves, and that includes our mistakes and sins. It is a time of nourishment for mind and soul, especially in the ministry of the Word. It is a time of adoration, of penitence and of forgiveness, and of reconciliation in the Peace. Above all, it is a time when we remember the last hours in the life of our Lord, when we obey his last command, and, in spirit, cross the centuries to share the Last Supper with him and his friends. For those old people who have suffered much in their lives, it may not be easy, at first, to think of the agony and the love of the crucifixion. But we can start simply, by being thankful for them, by wanting to understand them better and by trying to see how our own pain can be taken up into them. Then there is a time of great joy as the congregation proclaims:

> Christ has died
> Christ has risen
> Christ will come again.

The joy surges as the priest says the final prayer and reminds us that our Lord has 'brought us home' and 'opened for us the gate of glory'.

Although Cranmer's English had always been for me the

most beautiful language on earth, I quite soon found myself dropping into the swing of the new Alternative Service Book liturgy and enjoying it. In our church there is a combination of dignity, unobtrusive efficiency and yet homeliness that make it easy to worship God, and sometimes a strong feeling of spiritual love surges up from the congregation. Gradually, step by step, I have learned to move nearer to God through the service, and sometimes, during the following week, I use the hymns we have sung for quiet thought and meditation. I have about a mile to walk to the shops, and from the earliest days I have used that walk for repeating and 'praying' hymns or for saying short repetitive phrases.

Going up to the altar and coming back to the pew takes only a few minutes. Yet it is possible to make a prayer for the people at one's side or for our own needs and distresses and for those of our friends. It is a deeply personal and loving time, but I should say plainly that I have never had what people call 'mystical experience'. But I do have a strong sense of the nearness of the Lord who called his disciples to his last supper, and washed their feet before they ate, and died for them and the whole world on the following day.

It may not be easy to accept everything in this service. Some people are embarrassed by the Peace. In our church it is a double handshake, accompanied by the words, 'The peace be with you'. In it we recognize each other as brothers and sisters in Christ and are encouraged to show warmth of feeling. I am often very cheered by the glint in somebody's eye which says, 'I like you and I am glad you are here'. And a bear hug or a kiss will emphasize the message. I have learned to let myself go and accept other people's kindness expressed in physical touch. Each time it happens I am given a quiet happiness and confidence. It is immensely worthwhile to try to pass this on however shy we may be – though we may occasionally be rebuffed.

Then there may be mental reservations about the Creed. I find it an act of good manners to join in everything even though the intellect may not march wholly with what is being said.

27

When we go to a party in a friend's house, we accept the taste, the family practices and the forms of behaviour in that home, even though they are different from our own ways. A good-mannered participation in what the church is doing can do us no harm. We may very well come in time to a clearer under-standing of things we have questioned or to be able to make up our minds on some conundrum.

Some old people will certainly prefer a less sacramental form of service. All the Nonconformist churches will meet this need and usually offer a greater measure of congregational participa-tion in worship and organization. We should seek whatever suits our own individual temperament and taste, and we should try to find a church where we can be psychologically and phys-ically comfortable as well as spiritually at home.

But all kinds of people outside the church are also our companions and we must include them in our prayers. A baby has recently come into my family circle and he will be brought up a Mohammedan but he is one of the first people to be included in my prayers. There are many good long-term friends whose kindness and service to their neighbours can put my practice of Christianity to shame, but I doubt whether they will ever be praying people or members of a church. But they help me to grow in love and tolerance just as church people do, and they play an important part in my prayers. I also believe that everyone we have known in the past, people who are now dead, are a part of the great communion of saints and of our continuing life. Anyone for whom this idea is no help can leave such matters to God's wisdom and mercy. He knows and understands everything and there is no need to get stuck in argumentative matters. But many old people do want to think through the deep things of faith as far as they can and indeed now have the time to do this.

Everyone we meet is a companion on this journey. They are all a part of God's creation, which is loving and positive. Even mentally defective people have many ways of showing affection and trust. We owe them care and cherishing, and when we give it, we escape from our own self-centred being into God's love and that means that we are learning to pray.

This is how George Appleton suggests we pray for others in love:

O Thou source of all love,
let Thy love go out to all created beings,
to those I love and to those who love me,
to the few I know and to the many I do not know,
to all of every race,
to all the living in this world
and to all the living dead in the next world:
may all be free from evil and harm
may all come to know Thy love
and find the happiness of loving Thee and their fellows.
O let the small love of my heart
go out with thine all embracing love
for the sake of him who first loved us
and taught us love, even Jesus Christ our Lord.[2]

Now we have to think about the needs of those who cannot go to church because of physical disability. Some may be ill all the time and bedridden. There may be some, too, who are very reluctant to start a new habit of going regularly to church in old age and for whom it would be a real strain. I am sure it is a good thing to make the effort if one possibly can, and it will be deeply rewarding, but any serious strain will only destroy the will and the power to pray. There is a big difference of course between the newly retireds and those in their late seventies and eighties. Most newly retireds will be able to consider a regular commitment in church-going and perhaps to have some fairly definite rule for their prayer life. But for those of seventy-five or over, there should be no feeling of negligence or guilt about reluctance to go to church, or about any other practices or commitments. Church people tend to pay compliments to old people who achieve marathons or records of

2. George Appleton, *One Man's Prayers*. S.P.C.K. 1967.

church attendance, and certainly any activity cheerfully maintained is good for the health of both body and soul. But if we start competing with others in church attendance, or insist on attaining records, we shall kill all genuine prayer. God does not want this kind of thing from us. He wants our love and our readiness to turn to him and to listen to him, and nothing that impedes that flow of love should be attempted. A simple, loving relationship is within the power of us all.

But it is good to have the support and interest of other Christians. Many towns and churches have visitors' organizations and arrange for active newly retireds to help those who are ten or twenty years older. A letter or phone call to a vicar or minister would lead to a call from someone willing to help in this spiritual adventure and in other ways, too. But the sharing of spiritual experience is not always easy, even for the Christian who has been practising his faith for long years. Perhaps a good way is first of all to share some neighbourliness, to offer a cup of coffee, play a game of scrabble or dominoes, or show family photographs. It may be possible to share a radio or television service, and some churches have tapes of sermons or lectures on religious subjects. To listen to something of this kind together can lead to a gospel reading together and then perhaps to a short time of sharing prayers.

I lent the beautiful service of Compline to one bedridden ninety-year-old who had a feeling for lovely words and was still very active in her mind. She always wanted to read it with me even if it was the middle of the morning when I called. It is a moving service to read aloud, even if one is alone. It contains beautiful phrases like, 'Into thy hands I commend my spirit,' and, 'Keep me as the apple of an eye'. If I cannot get to church when I am under the weather I like to read the Holy Communion service, or perhaps Matins, at approximately the time that it is being said in church.

Most of us, after we are about seventy-five, experience increasing loneliness. Friends die, others become housebound, or find travelling difficult. People find us less interesting, and so friends come to see us less frequently. This makes life less interesting and exciting. There may be a deeper loneliness that we find difficult to communicate. We know that very soon we shall have no part in this world and so it becomes very precious. How can we bear to leave the ever changing beauty of the landscape from the kitchen window, that lovely willow tree through which the sunlight falls like drops of golden rain, the garden we have created over the years with love and care, the sitting-room on which we have implanted our personality and the little gifts all round the room, each representing a friendship. Will there be someone to help us when the time comes or shall we have to make the journey quite alone? If we still have our marriage partner, the unspoken question is often there – which of us will go first?

We can talk freely to God about these fears and depressions. We should try to listen to his loving reassurance as we find it perhaps in Psalms 46 or 23, in the first few verses of St John's Gospel, chapter 14, or in the wonderful end of the eighth chapter of the Epistle to the Romans.

On the whole subject of loneliness there is an inexpensive pamphlet (published by the Sisters of the Love of God at Fairacres in Oxford) called *From Loneliness to Solitude*. It is by Roland Walls, and is a reproduction of some short talks broadcast in 1975. In it the author speaks of the painfulness of loneliness, which is an experience of emptiness, and suggests that turning from loneliness to solitude is a turning from death to life. This is because in solitude we can make the discovery of our true selves. There is no strain or play-acting and we are free to open the door of our hearts to our Lord as he says, 'Behold I stand at the door and knock.'

Roland Walls also suggests a very simple practice I have found helpful. It is to read very slowly a page or two of a gospel with complete attention as though it is specially written for, and being specially addressed to, the reader. We can imagine that Jesus is speaking directly to us. I usually find that a page or two is not necessary; a few verses are enough.

It sometimes happens that before long we know that we have a friend in the room, someone standing very close to us. We can talk to him. We can break down and cry in his arms. We can share a joke with him. We can say anything we like and we can lean on his strength when all our own is ebbed away. Even if not a single word is framed, we can hold out our hands to him in love and know that we are praying. In old age we must accept that often we shall have strength for no more than that and it is all he wants.

We shall also create in ourselves a thirst for prayer which will have to be regularly quenched. Here is a simple prayer related to this thought:

> Dear Lord, I open my heart to your coming. Come close to me, Lord, and let me yield my whole being to you. Teach me to know myself and to fill my empty being with the radiant life of your love, that I may become a fountain of blessing to quench my own thirsts and to offer Love to meet the thirsts of my companions on this journey to you.

At first our prayer concentrates on ourselves. It has to be that way because we have a relationship to establish. But if we continue to let the relationship grow, we shall naturally and without any difficulty begin to pray for those we love. Then we shall find out that this is not enough and we shall start to pray for those we find it hard to forgive. The next step will be to realize that there are some who find it difficult to forgive us. It will all happen naturally and step by step, if we open ourselves to God's Holy Spirit. All the time there are new companions in our journey of prayer even though we may not meet them in the flesh.

Then we shall go on to pray for people all over the world whom we have never seen and especially for children deprived of shelter, of food and parents. We shall pray for saints like Mother Teresa who care for them. If only our growing hosts of people could do this for a short period each day, we could build up great reservoirs of love and power that flow from prayer.

Often during church intercessions, a prayer is offered for those who have no one to pray for them. It is a reminder that there are very great numbers of people who are unloved and uncared for, whose circumstances have made them incapable of seeking the good things of life. We may not be able to give practical love and care, but we can give our thought to them and offer them to God in our prayers. There are many, like homeless drug victims, whom life has battered so heavily, that they are incapable of prayer. There are those incapable of thought because of serious accident or disease, those deprived of family relationships from their earliest days who become afraid to love and trust, those who are the puppets of cruel men, those who are the victims of such continued twists of ill fortune that they are denied hope. If we are fortunate people who know affection for and trust in others, let us in gratitude remember the unhappy ones frequently, and ask God in his mercy to bring them to himself.

3

Seeking Help in the Life of Prayer

Since prayer is the main part of a relationship with God, elderly people who have known many happy relationships during their lives may need little help to grow into the most wonderful relationship of all. For many there will be a quiet natural growth and enjoyment of conversation with a friend who can be loved and trusted. We shall simply have to remember that God is always there, waiting for us, ready to pray with us and within us. We shall move naturally from thanking him and showing our needs, to prayer for others, and then perhaps to the prayer of silence, to wordless adoration and communion. It is the desire and the will that matter, not the methods nor the aids, though these things can help us.

But in all personal relationships, there may be periods of quiescence, of halting, perhaps even of regression and real difficulty. The will and the desire may need prompting, encouragement, strengthening. This has certainly been my experience even in a short period of five years.

Regular public worship in a lively and kindly church family is my main help to prayer but it is not necessary for everybody. Hermits can develop a rich spiritual life without it and so can bedridden invalids. Saints in concentration camps in the last war grew courageously to an ever-increasing awareness of God. But public worship prevents my own prayer from becoming too self-centred and it gives new insights to my private prayer, especially into directing my emotions into worship and adoration.

The second important support for one's own private prayer is someone with whom one can talk freely, perhaps even pray freely. For a beginner in old age, I would suggest someone who has had a quite long experience of the ups and downs of a life of prayer. And especially someone who will be understanding and forgiving, as God is, of the fact that we have neglected him for so many years.

For some people a spiritual director who is kindly and understanding will be an invaluable help in assuring us that we are really forgiven. We shall not pray with confidence nor get on with the demands of the present until we are assured of forgiveness for the mistakes and sins of the past. I am very fortunate, for my introspective miseries about the past are met with great kindness and understanding and are counterbalanced by a cheerful outgoing temperament. But it is not so easy for everyone. Some may have difficulty in finding a priest or minister who understands their need. For unspoken problems often take time to surface and some people take much longer to reach the point where they know that they want forgiveness. All priests today have to meet multifarious demands and responsibilities that leave them with virtually no free time at all. If you need spiritual advice and counsel, you must speak up for it. Your request will be met. But do not expect all your problems to be solved nor your heartaches healed in one interview. It is no easy matter to try to read another's heart and mind and to turn it in God's direction. The man or woman who seeks counsel should try sometimes to give as well as to get, for this is a relationship of trust and friendship though admittedly an uneven one. We, who are learning, must be content to do most of the taking.

And we must make up our minds what we want to take. If simply advice and counsel and an opportunity to unburden ourselves, we should say so. But if sin is worrying us, it is a most healing practice to clean it out in confession and so to make more room for God and for his will for us. Again, we must make up our own minds whether we might find it easier to receive God's forgiveness through the ministry of the church or through direct private prayer. The priest or minister will be infinitely kind and not hurry anyone until enough confidence comes naturally to say what we have to say. But in chapter 5, when we consider the mistakes and sins of the past, we will think further about this helpful practice of accepting spoken forgiveness.

Apart from the blessing of an understanding spiritual director, I am also fortunate in one or two good friends with whom I can talk fairly freely about this subject of prayer. But it is almost impossible to have complete understanding with another human being, and this is something we should not expect. We are all trying to walk with God in our own individual way and perhaps God sometimes withholds human understanding in order that we may turn more firmly to him. Even the great St Teresa of Avila was constantly complaining of the timidity or ignorance or conventionality of the men who advised her. Her spiritual flights could be so intense that her directors must have been scared stiff and incapable of advice, while she herself was lonely and worried in paths of which no one seemed to have any experience.

The Abbé de Tourville, too, constantly urged those who sought his help not to be afraid to rely on their own judgement and intuition.

Let us be able to depend quietly on ourselves. Let us gladly judge for ourselves which things most help, guide and teach us by observing the degree in which they fit our own particular temperament . . . when we are being true to ourselves we are in the best relationship we can reasonably expect to be with everything else.[1]

St Teresa found help in books, and said that she seldom went to her time of prayer without a book to fall back on, if necessary. And I think that books are my chief individual support in this life of prayer and they come second in importance to the service of the Eucharist. They are always to hand and they

1. Abbé de Tourville, *Letters of Direction*. Amate Press (Mowbray) 1982.

are full of the distilled wisdom and love of the saints who adventured along their own individual journey with God.

My books are a pretty varied lot and I make frequent use of libraries. To sum them up briefly they are my Bible, the 1928 Prayer Book, the Alternative Service Book, the works of a number of mystics, collections of prayers, books about prayer, hymn books, poetry, and theology of all kinds. Novels and plays, too, can offer facets of life that can turn the mind to our deepest needs and intuitions, and so to God. Two modern plays, *The Flashing Stream* by Charles Morgan and *The Dark is Light Enough* by Christopher Fry, are plays that have helped me to grow both intellectually and spiritually.

I seldom read any chapter of the gospels without finding some thought or phrase that will stay with me for a considerable time if I so wish. Once, when I read the story of Jesus walking with the two men to Emmaus, I was struck by the beauty of the simple words in St Luke's Gospel 24:29, 'Abide with us for it is towards evening and the day is far spent.' I made a three-word prayer, 'Abide with me,' from the first phrase and managed to shut out the remaining words of the famous hymn and also Wembley Cup Final scenes, though that's a television programme I can't bear to miss. I found that I was able to say this prayer quietly and lovingly for many weeks and at almost any time of day that I was alone. Such very simple prayers, offered in love, repeated over and over again can become a part of our unconscious, and enrich our whole being, and can also bring our dear Lord into our homes to share the everyday events of our lives. Other phrases that might help us are: 'Behold, I stand at the door and knock'; 'Ask and it shall be given you'; 'I am the Bread of Life'.

The Psalms, too, can be a frequent source of help. Many elderly people have heard the Psalms sung in Church Sunday by Sunday and know some of them almost by heart. It is a good thing to memorize phrases to hold on to when reading is difficult. In Psalm 103 there are so many lovely thoughts. One is, 'Like as a father pitieth his children'. I often use this when I pray for others whom I know to be in distress and say quite

simply, 'Be a father to her, Lord, comfort her and protect her.'
But this business of praying with the Bible is a tremendous
subject and a continually enriching practice. One of the best
modern books on the subject is George Appleton's *Praying
with the Bible.*

I think my favourite collection of prayers is an old-fashioned
one called *Great Souls at Prayer.* It was first published at the
end of the last century. It covers prayers written over fourteen
centuries, mostly by saints and famous Christian writers. There
is a prayer for each day of the year or sometimes two shorter
ones. They are very varied in content and in phrasing. If something modern is more acceptable, something very much in tune
with daily life and routines, perhaps the collections of prayers
by Frank Topping might meet the need. His *Lord of the
Morning* and *Lord of the Evening* reflect all kinds of moods
and experiences, joy, irritation, envy, depression, contentment,
trust and doubt. In these books one can often find a thought
that can be chewed over for several days.

Archbishop Ramsey's *Be Still and Know* is a little book that
could be helpful to any beginner. It suggests many ways of
developing the life of prayer.

Sooner or later we are all compelled to meditate on the
central fact of our faith. We shall want to read the story of the
crucifixion and resurrection in love and devotion and to know
our own personal involvement and responsibility. How soon
we come to such a slow, thoughtful and prayerful reading after
we start to pray will depend on our own personalities and
circumstances. But going throughout Holy Week to services in
a good church will draw us to the cross in our own way and
because of our own personal need and love. The thought and
worship can be continued along with the reading in our own
home. If we cannot go to church in Holy Week it may be
possible to set aside a time each day to read the passion story
from the gospels, especially from the Gospel of St Mark. This
should be a time for quiet, slow reading and for silent looking
and loving.

There is one very good book of prayers for anyone who

wants to learn to pray at the foot of the cross. It is Milner White's *Procession of Passion Prayers*.[2] Here are some of the prayers:

O God, our salvation and truth, grant that we thy children, rejecting the proud wisdoms of the world, may betake ourselves to the Cross of thy dear Son, to walk by its way, to repose in its shadow, to venerate its mercy, and to embrace its scorn; through the same Jesus Christ our Lord.

O Lord Jesus Christ, we beseech thee,
  touch us with those hands of thine,
    which thou didst suffer to be nailed to the Cross,
to bear the weight of the body of thy death, and of our sin;
  and in touching forgive, revive, and renew us;
    for thine endless mercies' sake.

O Lord Jesus Christ,
impart to me that trust of thine,
unquestioning, complete,
wherewith upon the very Cross
thou didst tranquilly commend thy spirit to thy Father;
that, whatsoever betide, I may recline
in the same everlasting arms;
for thine endless mercies' sake.

I sometimes think there are more books about prayer than about any other subject under the sun and, here I am, adding to the number. It certainly is not easy to choose from the infinity of books on a subject that is of the utmost importance, but in different ways, to every Christian. And my time for getting to know them has been limited.

People who have a feeling for the classics of prayer could be helped by reading a biography of St Teresa and her *Interior Castle*, or by Julian of Norwich's *Revelations of Divine Love* or St Francis de Sale's *Introduction to the Devout Life*. The *Cloud of Unknowing*, by an anonymous fourteenth century

2. E. Milner White, *Procession of Passion Prayers*. S.P.C.K. 1951.

writer, is by a saint who was very far advanced in the journey to God and yet kept his or her feet firmly rooted in common sense.

But most of us will want something with a more modern flavour and rather easier to read and understand. I find George Appleton and Sheila Cassidy not only experts in the life of prayer but deeply understanding of other people's needs and problems. Their books are to be found on almost every church and cathedral bookstall, and religious bookshops stock them. Their substance and their style are pleasurable and straightforward and not difficult to understand. There is plenty of solid material in them for both thought and practice.

Books that are, perhaps, a little more difficult, but which I have found immensely helpful are works by Father Christopher Bryant, Neville Ward, Harry Williams and Anthony Bloom. I have found books by Christopher Bryant and Neville Ward so enthralling that I have not been able to put them down but have thrown everything else to the winds until the book was finished. I am told that this is a very bad way to treat a book on such a serious subject. It should be 'read' and 'slowly tasted' rather like sucking a lozenge, but greed for books and experience has always been a weakness with me. Some of the works of the authors named above are listed in the notes at the end of this book.

I cannot refrain from mentioning my own favourite book, and since I have heard it recommended by three religious broadcasters, I know I am not alone in enjoying this very simple but very profound little book.

It is a translation of the Abbé de Tourville's *Letters of Direction*, a small paper-backed book that can be easily slipped into the pocket or handbag. It was written by a man confined to a sick bed for most of his life and yet it is the healthiest, the most bracing and the most understanding of all the books I have read about the spiritual life. This is what Evelyn Underhill says of him:

For the Abbé, life as seen from a sick room was inherently

splendid. It had its struggles, its pains, its obscurities, but . . . it poured forth from the heart of God and led man back again to God, often by rough, mountain tracks which we must accept, like the Swiss, as the normal means of communication.

She stresses the Abbé's teaching that it is 'inevitable that we shall stumble and sometimes fall into puddles, but we must take these things as they come and always go forward'.

The Abbé emphasized an idea that we started with in this little book – 'Just as I am'. He writes, 'We are to take ourselves as we are and offer ourselves as we are to the purposes of God.' And again,

The greatest saints have always shown the perfect combination of nearness to Our Lord on the one hand and a deep sense of their own unworthiness on the other. We should like to love our Lord perfectly: but the only perfect way is to love Him in a simple, human way. I assure you that it is a very excellent way, and, in the eyes of the angels, a most perfect and touching sight.

This sounds very easy and simple – and perhaps it is if we have a straightforward, trusting nature – but it means trying to bring the love and the will of our Lord for us into every detail of our everyday life. For independent, self-willed people, that is not easy. We just have to pick ourselves up every time we fail, and try again, and be ready to accept forgiveness.

Here is one of my favourite paragraphs from the Abbé's book which explains this a little further:

This is what our Lord asks of you . . . to be content to live with Him without anxiety, without any strain after perfection. Rest content with the knowledge that He is in His own person . . . in your soul, substantially, really, literally, that He does everything with you from the humblest duties to the highest. Your whole devotional life should consist in this companionship, accepted without ceremony, without intellectual or emotional effort, . . . and enjoyed in calmness and tranquillity. You are to say nothing to Our Lord except that which comes of itself, and in the most homely words. Never stop to ask whether you are worthy of this simple companionship, simply practise it, that is all. As for the other acts of external devotion, they are only patterns superimposed on this simple friendship. They should neither ruffle nor disturb its inward life.

Most Christians find that one of the best ways to progress in a life of prayer is to make a retreat. The purpose of a retreat is to get away from the clamours of everyday life into an outer and inner stillness and to know a stronger sense of the closeness of our Lord. Many parishes arrange at least one retreat each year which lasts for a few days and is conducted by an experienced leader, sometimes a priest who will take Eucharists and preach short homilies around a chosen theme. This can take place in a diocesan retreat house, often a most comfortable place in pleasant surroundings where the accommodation is good and cheap.

There are also many religious houses in this country which take guests who want to live a life approximating to that of the community and to spend their time in silence, meditation and prayer. It is usually possible to talk over problems at retreats, to receive spiritual advice or to make a confession and accept forgiveness.

There is a very helpful little book by Sister Joanna Baldwin[3] which gives a lot of information and help about retreats. But almost any parish priest will be able to give information. Sister Joanna gives some excellent advice:

It is a one-sided relationship if one party does all the talking . . . you may find words a distraction and that you need to develop a more contemplative form of prayer . . . Bring before God the person you really are. If you are angry, sad, bored, anxious or happy, tell God and use your feelings as

3. Sister Joanna Baldwin, *Learning about Retreats*. Mowbray 1982.

part of your prayer. Do not try to disembody yourself and become pure spirit because it does not work.

There is an association for giving information and advice about Retreats. It is the Association for Promoting Retreats, Church House, Newlon Road, London W2 5LS. Its journal is called *Vision*.

Sometimes I arrange a one-day retreat for myself in my own home. As I grow older and find packing bags and travelling more of a chore, I think this is something I may do more frequently. I just give up the usual household duties and shopping, and spend the time in reading, meditation and prayer which includes silence. I plan for the day and make it one of enjoyment; it is a small holiday with our Lord.

There has to be a theme or a book to which to relate thought and prayer or, if one cannot get to church, the services for the week in the Anglican Alternative Service Book (A.S.B.) provide plenty of material. Once I had a day in which I gave thanks for the new spiritual life in my old age and for the people who had helped me to it. I tried to analyse what had happened and what had led to it. We are often very blind when we try to get to know ourselves but I think it is good to make the effort.

If I arrange a day retreat, five hours is more than enough when I am alone, with short breaks for a meal or a bit of gardening or knitting. I choose a meal that is a small treat, though simple, like a jacket potato with lots of butter and tangy Cheddar cheese. Very bad for the figure but not for the soul. It is a day of rest and happiness, a day of thankfulness, a day in which I try to know my Lord's presence in my little house and his forgiveness and love for me.

A retreat gives an opportunity for some spiritual reading. The Fairacres publication group in Oxford has a long list of inexpensive pamphlets written by good authorities on the devotional life, many of whom are experienced in taking retreats. The Church Literature Association of Tufton Street, London can provide similar helpful pamphlets; one of the best is by

Christopher Bryant, *Why Prayer?* It is a summary of material used in some of his lengthier works.

Sometimes radio and television programmes can give impetus for thought and prayer. I especially like the early Sunday service, 'The Shape of God'. Frequently the gospel and the theme of the week in the A.S.B. are opened up and there is a thought that can be carried into the morning Eucharist, developed there and reflected on throughout the week. Many old people enjoy hearing old-fashioned favourite hymns as well as modern ones in Sunday hymn singing. Few can resist the happiness of Thora Hird's programmes in the summer. Clearly she loves singing hymns, she loves God, and she loves people, and just to listen to such an uninhibited, outgoing personality can hardly fail to do us good.

For the newly retired and for those who are still quite energetic in body and mind one great help to a life of prayer could be a definite, simple Rule. That is, one could promise to give to God each day a definite time and usually about the same time of day. But as we grow older we grow forgetful, and we have more 'off days'. A sense of guilt about such a Rule can do no good at all, so always promise rather less than you think you can manage and if it is possible to increase and develop the time, then it is a happy thing to do so. If we know we have been plain slack and careless, then simply say so to our Lord, and ask his forgiveness and start again. It could be possible for a lot of people to promise about ten minutes at the start of the day and perhaps twenty minutes later. But it has also become one of my joys to talk to our Lord at almost any time of the day just for a minute or two in the middle of anything I am doing. I may share a letter with him or a fear or a worry, or talk to him about a friend in distress, say 'Thank you' for the kindness that leaves a gift on my doorstep. I can share a joke, a funny situation or a good meal. This helps me to be sure that he is there all the time, interested in all that concerns me. But it is good to have a definite allotment of time, too, and most of us will come to look forward to it and think of it not as a duty, but as a time of relaxation and joy. Whenever during this regular time of prayer we have a special sense of the nearness of our Lord it is good to write or frame a sentence or two of thanksgiving. Such thoughts may help us in times when it is perhaps more difficult to trust and love. Here is a short prayer I wrote during an Easter season:

My Lord, my Master, my Friend whose never failing love conquered sin and death, I love you and adore you. I bless you for the renewal and resurrection of this lovely spring day. I ask that the love from which your resurrection sprang may awaken my heart to love you more dearly and follow you more nearly.

4

Enjoying Prayer

'Goodnight dear. Remember to say your prayers.' Then a good-night kiss. The light switched off and the door closed. Or, if we were still scared of the dark and somebody understood, left ajar, so that we could hear the comforting to-ing and fro-ing downstairs.

And did we say our prayers? I doubt it. More than likely we fumbled for those toffees we had hidden in some secret corner of a drawer and then cogitated if we could swop our thrush's eggs for John's penknife tomorrow. Saying our prayers was a vague kind of duty which had no real meaning at all – birds' eggs and penknives can be seen and have value. But the Almighty was some kind of vague, powerful Being, always too ready to swoop on you for being naughty. He certainly would not approve of toffees after teeth had been cleaned. He was altogether associated with duty and there was more than enough of that at school.

Such crude, childish concepts can persist, unquestioned, through the working years of our lives. Occasionally, some stark reality, like a road accident to a beloved child, or the onset of cancer for the person we love most and can't do without, may force us to beseech the Almighty to reverse the reality. But usually events take their remorseless course – or so it seems, and we decide that prayer 'does not work'.

But in old age, with much adult experience behind us, there is time and enough intuition to begin to discover what prayer really is. If we can even recognize its many-sided nature, and start to experience the love of our Lord, we shall discover a growing joy.

We may have already understood that God is taking the initiative and that we are being helped to form a relationship with him. Perhaps we think of him, as Abraham must have done, as a Being who is all-knowing, all-loving, all-powerful. This is true for most Christians today. But in talking to some happy and contented old people, I find they express it in very simple ways. One said to me, 'Prayer is talking to my great Friend. He is my Creator; he gives life and all the gifts we enjoy. I find I am closest to him in my garden, when I can sit quietly and just look at an apple tree in blossom or watch a mother bird teaching her young to feed themselves. That is when I am bound to thank him for his goodness.' When I spoke of the evil in the world, in such sharp contrast with the peace of her garden, she answered, 'Yes, I think about the threat of evil and try to face the fact that atomic power can destroy even the grass and the weeds. Yet I can trust him that all the infinite variety of Creation in my garden must somehow triumph in the end over destruction. My prayer is simply trust in this Love and my prayer comes most naturally out of doors when God's creative voice seems to be praying inside me.'

We have so far spoken of a journey towards God. We could now begin to think of it as a movement of our self into God, and of opening our own self so that God can penetrate it.

I first saw this joy in operation during the 'Celebration Fortnight' in our town. I think the Franciscan team, who were running it, were more full of joy than any other group of people I have ever met. They were certainly not free from pressures, heartaches, psychological problems, difficult decisions to be taken and loneliness. But their joy stemmed from their relationship with God. As far as I could see, they were in love with him, and this love – if love is the right word – swamped all the problems and difficulties I have just mentioned. They wanted us to fall in love with God, to 'catch' him, as it were, as one catches an infection. And I caught the infection.

On the last evening the leader of the campaign made a surprising statement. He said, 'There aren't any sins, there's just one sinful state – self-centredness.' There are few of us who have not had to admit to a fair degree of self-centredness at some time in our lives and I certainly am no exception. I felt I had to take up this challenge and try to move, over and over again, away from self-centredness into God-centredness. It is often a case of one step forward and two steps backwards but at least I am beginning to know just a little of the joy I have 'caught'. And very rarely, it comes flooding in like a great torrent.

All this will sound very much in the clouds to people who have to be very practical in their old age just to cope with the struggle of continuing to exist and to pay their way. But just before our Celebration began, we were given a pamphlet which expressed the hopes of the organizers, and I felt my mind and heart attuned to their thought. They wrote, 'When we decided to call our special fortnight a "Celebration" we meant just that. We mean it to be a fortnight of enjoyment and happiness in discovering. It's easy to think of Christian faith as being about morality, restrictions, giving up, discipline, whereas what it's really about is gratitude, joy, fun and giving. God is wonderful to know.'[1]

The key thought for me in that loving message was 'God is wonderful to know'. If we can start or finish our prayers with that thought in mind, the wonder and the joy will grow in us, maybe very quietly and imperceptibly, but it will happen. We shall put on a new kind of being where God is allowed to possess the centre with his joy, and that leaves no room for self-centredness. It will not happen in a moment of time but very gradually, as we pray. There will probably be many occasions of slipping back into self-centredness.

'But how?' someone will be murmuring. It is not easy to be definite and practical because we do have to 'catch' this joy through opening our hearts and trying to shed our inhibitions about being good. Or even doing good, though one of the results of Franciscan joy is a tremendous concern for the neigh-

1. Brochure for 'Celebration Fortnight', St Peter's Church, Petersfield. 1978.

bour. The truest way is to look at our Lord and to love him, and for this we usually need time and silence. It has helped me much to go into old churches and to sit and try to feel the Christian joy that has been poured into the building over the centuries. In one of her plays Dorothy Sayers says of Canterbury Cathedral, 'Prayer had soaked into the very stones.' After a time, many people find that it is a help to concentrate on the crucifix. And again, after a time, joy will flow from it.

The crucifixion was an event in time, but it is also an event in eternity because through it God showed to each one of us a love that would endure shameful humiliation, desertion and painful death. Suffering, betrayal, abandonment, rejection are things we all experience sometime in our life and from which we shrink. But through the cross, God shows us that he knows these things, that he is at the very heart of them and that from them we can let our love flow as he let his love flow for the whole world. And in that love is joy.

Another way to know joy in prayer is to wait on God in silence. This may sound very easy but it can sometimes be more difficult than holding a conversation with God. For all kinds of thoughts, memories, clamours will come crowding into the silence. Sometimes the thoughts are casual enough and they can be quietly pushed away. But some can be deeply rooted resentments, angers, jealousies, inadequacies, fears. It is an opportunity to speak them out or at least to feel them honestly and try to understand some of their roots. Then they can be handed over with confidence to our Lord who understands their nature fully. As we hand them over, one by one, his peace and joy can take their place.

If it is very difficult indeed to give up the unhappy feelings, then perhaps it is also best for a time to give up the silence, too, and to say frequently some simple sentence, concentrating on it, and putting our love into it, as for example, 'My soul waiteth upon God; from him cometh my salvation.' Or, 'In the shadow of thy wings will I rejoice.'

Though the deepest joy comes from looking and loving and from losing ourselves in God's love, there are many simple practical ways in which we can help ourselves to enjoy our prayer. One of the best is just to tell God at any moment of the day when something happens that gives us happiness. Happiness is not such a profound experience as joy; joy is a more spiritual emotion but happiness of all kinds, if expressed in gratitude, can help us to enjoy prayer. For example one of my great delights in winter is my open coal fire and I specially love the moment when the fire is newly lit and little tongues of flames are shooting up in all directions. Even in my childhood, I always called a fire with many tongues of flame a 'Holy Ghost fire' because I had seen a rather comic picture of the disciples standing in a neat semi-circle each with a tongue of flame sitting precisely on the centre of his head. I sometimes say, 'Let my spirit burn with love for you, Lord, as cheerfully as my fire burns.'

When the fire dies down in the evening, it is often possible to draw together seemingly dead coals, to create a little draught, and so to have a small fire of total clarity. My Father used to call it 'the sweetest bit of fire in the whole day'. So there is an opportunity for a joyful little prayer. 'Dear Lord, let my old age burn more sweetly in your love and service and give warmth to those who hold out their hands in need to me.' Needless to say my actions often fail to match the words of my prayer.

Those of us who are still fairly active can sometimes express enjoyment in prayer through physical movement. Many people can pray easily out of doors when they go for a country walk and some say that the physical activity of walking helps to create a rhythm of praise. It is natural to want to kneel or genuflect when offering adoration but adoration is an offering of love and worship and no physical movement is essential. Many young people today move their arms and bodies vigorously and rhythmically when singing choruses but I feel embarrassed if I try to do that. However, on a bad winter day with slippery pavements, when I have to stay indoors, I can happily play over tapes of lively hymns like 'Angel voices ever singing' or 'When morning gilds the skies' (even though it is snowing) and move with a dancing step round my dining-room table, singing in my croaky voice as I move. This combines exercise and praise and cheers up a day when I cannot go out. However badly one sings it is therapeutic to raise one's voice and try to hymn our God and Creator. I shall never forget my own joy and, I think, the joy of everyone else there, when, on a rather special day of Thanksgiving, I persuaded the whole congregation to get up out of their pews and join in a dance round the church to the wonderful hymn, 'Lord of the Dance'.

Whatever we specially like doing in these days of our retirement, let us try to be conscious of our joy in the doing, however simple it may be. So many love gardening, others making music, others fiddling with a bit of carving or learning to sketch or paint. Most women enjoy sewing or knitting, especially for grandchildren. And many of us catch up on reading for which there may have been little time in our working years.

Whatever it is, ask our Lord to share your joy and make some very short prayer to express happiness. One job I love is kneading bread, making a rhythm of it, and really punching, and I can nearly always think of a sentence to go with the rhythm as, for example, 'The eyes of all wait upon Thee; thou givest them their meat in due season'. George Herbert summed up the joy we can all find in simple work in a hymn which begins, 'Teach me my God and King, in all things Thee to see'. He expresses the joy in the famous two lines:

> Who sweeps a room as for Thy laws
> Makes that and th' action fine.

Enjoyment of music and poetry can be happily integrated with our prayer. Music often introduces people into another world altogether, so that they have a glimpse or feeling of eternity, a world in which place and time do not inhibit our emotions from seeing God with spiritual vision. I am not very musical myself; it is the music of words that speaks most powerfully to me. Nevertheless there have been times when music has moved me profoundly and has led me to prayer. The King's College carol service does this each year without fail; and I was certainly

carried into the experience of another world by the singing of
the St John Passion in Bath Abbey and by Wirral schoolgirls
singing 'Flocks in pastures green abiding'. The first time I heard
Berlioz' 'Shepherds' Song' from *The Childhood of Christ* I was
moved to tears. Music, then, seems to lead us into another
world, to make us aware of a spiritual dimension, in a way that
words so often fail to do. I am sure that enjoyment of music
can contribute to enjoyment of prayer. All true enjoyments fill
out the meaning of our gratitude.

For me it is enjoyment of poetry that so often becomes a
part of my prayer. I have a cassette of some of George
Herbert's poems most beautifully read by Jean Stell. When I
play that through, George Herbert and our Lord himself come
to the place where I am praying and if my heart is cold or
obstinate, it is immediately warmed into devotion. George
Herbert was a seventeenth-century country parson who
suffered much both physically and spiritually. Yet he could
always win through to joyful gratitude and praise in his poems.
Most hymn-books contain one of his poems, 'King of Glory,
King of Peace', in which he longs that every moment of his life
shall be given to joyful praise and prayer.

> Seven whole days, not one in seven,
>   I will praise Thee,
> In my heart, though not in heaven,
>   I can raise Thee,
> Small it is, in this poor sort
>   To enrol Thee;
> E'en eternity's too short
>   To extol Thee.

George Herbert knew, perhaps more than any other writer in
the English language, that no human being can have true peace
and rest of the heart until he seeks to know God. Many do not
know this; people have all kinds of aims and ambitions in their
lives, but Herbert knew that the true end of man is God. And
men's hearts are restless till they rest in God. He expresses this

in a famous poem, 'The Pulley'.[2] It is a poem that often appeals to the old who have shed most of their earthly ambitions.

> When God at first made man,
> Having a glass of blessings standing by:
> Let us (said he) pour on him all we can;
> Let the world's riches, which dispersed lie,
> Contract into a span.
>
> So strength first made a way;
> Then beauty flowed, then wisdom, honour, pleasure:
> When almost all was out, God made a stay,
> Perceiving that, of all his treasure,
> Rest in the bottom lay.
>
> For if I should (said he)
> Bestow this jewel on my creature,
> He would accept my gifts instead of me,
> And rest in Nature, not the God of Nature:
> So both should losers by.
>
> Yet let him keep the rest,
> But keep them with repining restlessness:
> Let him be rich and weary, that at least,
> If goodness lead him not, yet weariness
> May toss him to my breast.

There can be few people who have not, at some time, longed in weariness, to drop all care and responsibility, and to be carried in loving arms, like a child, where they long to be. Prayer can offer those loving arms and the peaceful strength that carries our weariness.

Music, poetry, great art, all these can move us to prayer and help us to enjoy it. There are, too, specific moments in our daily life, that can awaken joy in prayer. I have one that occurs most mornings as I leave my house to catch a bus to do my shopping or to walk into town. My father had a streak of

2. 'The Pulley' (sometimes entitled 'The Gifts of God') is included in the World's Classics edition of George Herbert's *Poems* (O.U.P.) and in Palgrave's *Golden Treasury*.

paganism in his Celtic make-up and the threshold of the home was of significance to him. I still stand for some moments as I go, with my foot half in and half out of my home, and give thanks for the world I am leaving behind, for the life of my home. Then I tip my foot forward on to the outside path and ask God's blessing on the experiences and the people I am going to meet during the next hour or so. Many of us can be greatly moved too, by the sunset light, especially the dying light of a calm summer evening, and it is good to remember the beautiful lines in Wordsworth's 'Evening on Calais Beach':

> The holy time is quiet as a nun,
> Breathless with adoration.

We can let joy in the beauty of the evening and joy in our adoration of the Creator of all beauty become a living part of our prayer.

Anniversaries mean much to me, especially the birthdays and the death days of people I have loved. There is a place, too, where I often remember them. It is a grassy patch between our church and a hut where we serve coffee. It is part of a one-time graveyard and on Sunday mornings, in the half hour before our service begins, there is no more peaceful place on earth and no better place to remember friends who are dead. The market place is only a stone's throw away and I can identify with the thinking of John Betjeman in a simple poem in which he expresses the joy that some people know in the communion of saints.

> Now when the bell for Eucharist
> Sounds in the Market Square,
> With sunshine struggling through the mist
> And Sunday in the air,
>
> The veil between her and her dead
> Dissolves and shows them clear
> The Consecration Prayer is said
> And all of them are near.[3]

3. 'House of Rest' in John Betjeman, *Collected Poems*. John Murray 1970.

We all have our own moments, our own places, our own memories of remembered love or tragedy, of deep spiritual significance for us. Moments and places where we have been close to God without knowing it at the time. Perhaps we do know it now in old age and, if so, let us give thanks and make joyful gratitude a part of our prayer.

This sense of joyful gratitude will be a very great help in our life of prayer. If only we yield to it, whenever possible, dwell on it, stretch it out, it is far and away the best medicine for the worries and fears of old age. And it is something far more than a medicine, it is a pathway to the love of God. It is a firm and yet gentle cord that binds us closely to him. It can be practised, learned and cultivated and perhaps at no time better than in old age when we have begun to understand more clearly the things that have true value for us. When we take a little grandson for a walk, and his hand sits trustingly in ours, and he talks of this and that and takes a lively delight in flowers and water and sand and trees and pussies and birds, this is a moment to say a profound 'Thank you' for all this innocent wonder and joy in God's world, a moment to draw close to God and to put the little boy into his arms. When we begin to knit yet another baby shawl for another expected grandchild, it is a moment for joy and thankfulness in our children and their children. When we take down the white stick because sight is beginning to fail and trundle along to the pub on a fine summer evening, and hear welcoming nonsense in the voices of our friends, let us enjoy our evening to the full and come back happy with gratitude for companionship and kindness. When a nurse in hospital relieves our pain efficiently and with reassuring words, we can offer our gratitude to God for all whose lives are devoted to the work of healing. When we know a terrible sense of loss as a wife or husband or good friend dies, we can fuse with the moments of desolation a thankfulness for the faithful love of past years. If we look ahead to our own deathbed, when we may be incapable of conscious thoughts, we can offer present thanks for that future moment when we shall be very close to our dear Lord.

Whenever we absorb ourselves into this kind of thankfulness, we shall come unconsciously close to God. It will be like the hug we exchange with dear ones when no words are spoken but silent understanding and trust are exchanged on both sides. In this kind of prayer of thankfulness, there is no need for words, just a giving of ourselves as we gave ourselves to another when we were in love.

John Byrom[4] says that is how the life of prayer should be – as though we are falling in love, in silence, in wonder and in tremendous joy and hope. Many old people do know an experience of falling in love but in a less emotional and serene way than in youth. I suspect it happened to Abraham and Sarah as it does happen to some old couples. Most old people keep it dark because the world can ridicule and be cruel. But both the saints and ordinary people have known this experience which enables them, as St Francis did, after his conversion, to see the world with new eyes. George Herbert summed it up, 'In age I bud again.' Falling in love with God and with people simultaneously can be like a new rose bush with two strong shoots each bearing a golden rose.

With most people there comes a time when being in love has to give way to the more solid and humdrum relationship of marriage. Humdrum it may be, but in effect it is a new kind of adventure away from emotional delights into solid trust, friendship and loyalty. If our life in God moves in that direction, and it is so for most people, then the old are the lucky ones. For they will have worked through that kind of experience on the human plane, or perhaps have made mistakes that they now understand and feel they could avoid. The old, armed with earthly experience of love and passion, and the intuitions that flow from the business of day-to-day living, can accept our Lord with a trust that may have been difficult in the early days of marriage. Looking back, we see more clearly the things for which we should have been profoundly grateful and to which

4. John Byrom, *Prayer, the Passion of Love*. S.L.G. Press, Fairacres, Oxford, 1981.

we were blind. And so we come back to that sense of joyful gratitude and of enjoying prayer. It can be a strong cord to bind us forever to God.

It is a good thing to try sometimes to express joy in prayerful words. This is one of my attempts:

For all the joy you have poured out on me, Lord, I praise you, bless you and adore you. For joy in my own being, in my body, mind and spirit. For joy in the knowledge of sins forgiven, for joy in all the prayer and longing to know you and love you, for joy that comes out of the acceptance of tensions, conflict, rejection and unhappiness. For joy in all the lovely people I know and in my learning with your help to pray for them, for joy in their kindness and integrity, for joy in their funny side and their odd little weaknesses and their readiness to laugh and be humble, for joy in their goodness shared with me and with others. For joy in the beauty of your world and its power to shape my worship and prayer, for the gentle hills that enfold my home, for the blue tits who daily to seek a small bounty, for the tall proud scarlet tulips and the scent of the lilac and the roses called Peace and Blessings that welcome me at my door. For all this abundance of joy, dear Lord, make me humble and glad and faithful. Grant me the insight to recognize those in whom no joy stirs and give me opportunities, love and courage to pour a little of your joy into their emptiness.

5

Difficulties

There are a few old people who seem never to grow old in spirit. The future continues to hold for them the exciting, the unknown, new paths to adventure. Hope still commands the twin fortresses of heart and mind. But for the majority of septuagenarians warning bells are ringing. Physical exertion has to be curtailed, mental activity slows down. Embarking on new personal relationships or activities requires a more conscious effort. All this is natural for the elderly, and almost universal experience. Zest for life may gradually ebb away and behind this dwindling of our powers lies the fact, so seldom spoken of, that death is not far distant.

So elderly people tend to live much more in the past than they formerly did, and usually to dwell on happy memories and to talk about them a great deal. Reminiscing may or may not be a bad habit of old people but it is a fairly inevitable development. Many of us find that our memory of what happened a week ago can be poor but memories of a quarter or half a century ago can be very vivid indeed. For the elderly who, in old age, accept a definite commitment to become a disciple of our Lord, the past can become a problem, even though there may be thousands of happy memories and a life-time of fruitful and selfless activity. The latecomer into the church is not always welcome, and will probably feel that he has failed our Lord during the best years of his life.

Both for the new disciple and for the long-term Christian, a good, honest look at the past can do no harm. I have met one very good teacher of prayer who suggested dividing up one's life into seven-year periods, consciously recollecting the special blessings of each period and then giving thanks for them. For some this may not be easy, for life is a whole, a flowing stream, sometimes meandering peacefully and happily, sometimes disturbed by eddies and unexpected currents. A neat design of life does not fit the experience of many people and in that case it may be better to go back to the simple words of the first chapter – 'Just as I am'. It will help us to recollect that God must have been accepting us, just as we are and forgiving us all through the years when we did not know him.

Nevertheless the fact of past sin and guilt may distress us. Yet an obsessive sense of guilt is wrong; it is stultifying and a denial of God's omnipotence and love. We have to look honestly at past sin and to love ourselves in spite of it. It is a weakness to concentrate too long on introspective self-examination. We can't forget the past; nor does God. But we can accept it and ask his forgiveness and so strengthen our relationship with him and our love for him. If God forgives us, as he always does when a sinner is penitent, then we, too, must do his will and forgive ourselves. If we have suffered unduly at the hands of others or through harsh circumstances, we must also forgive what these things have done to us. Then we can reach forward to the new growth that lies ahead of us.

There are many ways in which we can help ourselves to know God's forgiveness. One is to read the stories in the gospels of how Jesus dealt with sinners. A second is to experience the Sacrament of Reconciliation, at one time called 'going to Confession'. A third is to think seriously of some person or experience that has hurt us and to make a conscious effort of forgiveness. If we can maintain this for a few days we shall know that the act of forgiveness is steadily becoming more real and without doubt God's power of forgiveness is infinitely greater than ours.

In reading the stories of Jesus' dealings with sinners two things seem to recur. One is that, though he never minimized the sin, he never dwelt on it. He was interested in the sinner, not the sin committed. The second is that any sinner who showed the least longing to move into a new life, had his longing recognized. Jesus seemed to give himself wholly to that longing and to fill it with his spirit so that the mustard seed of longing could grow into a great tree.

I find the story of Zacchaeus (Luke 19:2–9) very compelling, perhaps because I do not myself reach five feet, but I doubt whether I should have managed to climb a tree to see Jesus. But I should certainly have been stirred to great joy when he invited himself to come to dinner. I love any excuse for a party and for cooking, and for such a guest my cup of joy would have overflowed. Surely Jesus laughed at a little man climbing a tree to see him and laughed, too, at the thought of dining at the house of Zacchaeus. Laughter and forgiveness go hand in hand. Possibly Zacchaeus at some time admitted his dishonesty and greed. But the attitude of Jesus to him was cheerful and full of hope. 'This day is salvation come to your house,' affirms Jesus. He made his future friendship plain by asking to dine with Zacchaeus, a sinner.

Similarly, Jesus did not condone the sin of the woman taken in adultery (John 8:3–11), but there is no discussion of it. Simply the firm command, 'Go and sin no more.' There is almost an element of the comic as the self-righteous men, prepared to stone a sinner, slink away from the man who was sinless.

This woman, assumed by many to be Mary Magdalene, became a saint of the Church and a friend of Jesus, because he refused to allow her emotional power to be handicapped by her past. The same kind of releasing experience was given to Peter after his betrayal. In the famous post-resurrection encounter of Jesus and Peter (John 21:15–17), Jesus briefly judged and condemned Peter by asking the heartbreaking question, 'Simon, son of Peter, lovest thou me?' But the question was not one of judgement only. It gave Peter the chance to reaffirm the love he had betrayed. At first he was almost too ashamed to do this. But by asking the question three times Jesus gave Peter the opportunity to wipe out his three acts of betrayal. Then he urged Peter forward, away from concentration on his sin, to get on with the work that he had to do for the Lord he had betrayed. The attitude of Jesus to sinners who repented was loving, demanding and creative.

But if there is still some evil memory that lurks within us and will not yield to the truth of these stories, it is wise to seek the advice and help that lie within the Sacrament of Reconciliation.

When we held the Celebration Fortnight in our church, the Sacrament of Reconciliation was beautifully portrayed in flowers in a flower festival related entirely to the sacraments. This is how the sacrament was explained:

> The wonder of God's love and forgiveness is the great spur to the Christian life and the source of joy and happiness. Nowadays many people seek the help of an experienced priest in living the Christian life and they value the spiritual counsel which is part of the Sacrament. They find it helpful to draw on the experiences of other Christians. Really to face up to oneself in the presence of God and confess those sins that nag at us, and then to hear the words that assure us of God's forgiveness is most wonderfully liberating and healing. Here God reconciles us to himself.[1]

In practice, it is never easy to reveal the worst of oneself to another human being. Not just the sins, but the mistakes and the weakness and the silliness. But it is a challenge and a small spiritual adventure and it certainly is liberating as the great psychiatrists know. It fosters spiritual growth, though perhaps only slowly. At first one often has to work through an adolescent sense of guilt which is not true and joyful penitence but seems to me to be a necessary stage on the way to penitence. I have been very fortunate to find a father-in-God who allows me to make my own stumbling way but is ready to give a hand if I need help. Just as we have to discover our own methods in prayer, so it is worth while to take trouble to find a spiritual director who suits our own temperament and needs.

1. Brochure for 'Celebration Fortnight', St Peter's Church, Petersfield. 1978.

A psychiatrist can also help us to face up to the past and find the way to forgiveness but most good psychiatrists know that a priest with experience of human weakness can often do this more effectively. There is a story that when Carl Jung, the great psychiatrist, visited a large mental institution, the head of the hospital said to him, 'If only I could persuade my patients that their sins are forgiven, quite half of them could go home tomorrow.' Both the head of the hospital and Carl Jung knew that an obsessive sense of guilt is the cause of much mental illness and distress. If only the patient can describe his sin and talk about his sense of guilt he usually comes to understand his need of pardon and is ready to accept God's forgiveness which can be spoken by a priest. The priest is not forgiving the sin but is speaking or mediating God's forgiveness. This mediation of priest or minister is not essential but it can be very reassuring. Sometimes a good, understanding friend can give similar help and assurance.

Father Bryant gives excellent advice to those seeking to know forgiveness either in their private prayers or in the Sacrament of Reconciliation. He stresses that the teaching of Jesus reveals sin as something negative. It is

> not so much the doing of what we ought not to do, but leaving undone what we ought to do. It is a missing the mark, a failure to pay our debts, a neglect of our talents and opportunities, an ignoring of the claims of others on our compassion, a refusal to forgive . . . Jesus sees it as a self-exclusion from the kingdom and an opting for death.[2]

Father Bryant distinguishes between the sins for which we know we are to blame and the bad moods, depressions and resentments for which we need healing rather than blame. We cannot always draw an accurate line between the two kinds of fault but we should try to do so and to realize that there is a distinction. He links confession with adoration. 'In both kinds

2. Christopher Bryant, *Why Prayer?* Hillingdon Papers, Church Literature Association, 1975 (out of print).

of confession, we open ourselves to the healing power of God, who is all the time at work within us.'

But we should not expect to achieve miracles through confession or any other kind of practice. Especially in old age we have to be prepared to move slowly and patiently towards our Heavenly Father, shedding perhaps a bit of egoism here, a bad habit there, freeing ourselves of a resentment at one time, and a fear at another, and so steadily leaving a little more room for the forgiveness and the power of God. In old age it will all happen very gradually unless we are quite exceptional people.

A difficult question for many people is to know how our individual sin is redeemed by the death of our Lord on the cross. Many who have a straightforward evangelical approach hold a simple faith that the sacrifice of Jesus was sufficient for the sins of the whole world. For others it can be difficult to understand how this can be. Gerald Priestland recently asked some of the theological experts in the country to give their point of view. But even they seemed to find this matter difficult and there was no consensus of opinion. I doubt whether intellect and reasoning can do much for us. My own experience is conditioned by emotion and experience, not by thinking. During the years when I held no formal religious faith, I was sometimes called on to endure strains and difficulties that I felt were too great for me. Though I had no clearly defined faith, I always turned to the cross and said to myself, 'If he endured that forsaken agony, then I can endure this little bit.' Even now, at times when I feel I have been betrayed or rejected, I become hard-hearted and turn away from the basic need in all good human relationships, the need to be vulnerable. Then in pride, I can cling to the hard-heartedness which makes me miserable. Very often there comes a moment – and I can't help thinking that God arranges it – when a generous letter is pushed through my letter-box or someone leaves a thoughtful present on my doorstep or an unexpected gift of flowers arrives. Then I have to give in and through the healing tears of surrender I always find myself holding out my hands to the cross. And I ask forgiveness, which in the emotional moment, I am quite sure comes from the cross. I think it is better to trust the emotional reaction than theological or intellectual arguments.

Harry Williams brings together in a most helpful way, prayer, sin and the cross. He says that 'there will be times when savage hatreds, smouldering anger, deadening depressions will intrude on our prayers'.[3] He goes on to say:

> Christ on the Cross was in conflict with all the destructive forces in the world, and by His Passion, He overcomes destructiveness and wins the day for creativeness. Christ sometimes invites us to share His conflict with Him. Our feelings of anger, worry, depression are signs that for the time being, Christ is calling us to stand with Him in the thick of the battle, to face within us the forces of destruction. And since it is with Christ that we are standing in the thick of the battle, although we will continue to feel bloody and bloody-minded, in deepest reality Christ's victory over destructiveness will be working itself out within us and by means of us.

I know a little of this unhappiness, for though I have wonderful friends in the Church we are human beings and it hasn't been all honey. Such spiritual growth as I have known often seems a thing of pathetic shreds and patches, of endless ups and downs. At one moment there can be profound spiritual happiness and new understanding and then suddenly the old ego is there with a childish outburst and harsh words. There can be co-operation with the new friends who are dear to me, and also resentments and dislikes plainly shown by others and I come home to think about 'I wish you would find another church, Miss Know-all.' There are a few worthwhile achievements but often in the face of opposition, and there is the quiet sharing with gentle souls in the life of prayer. There are moments of glory in the Eucharist and in services like the Vigil of Easter Eve; there are moments of despair when I cry, 'I can't go on, Lord, I can't.' There are moments of fierce temper

3. H. A. Williams, *Becoming What I Am*. Darton Longman and Todd 1977.

when an offering of writing is rejected, and there is a forgiveness for the outburst that reflects the forgiveness of God.

Most Christian people know about these things but to those who are hesitant to join a church because they know their own weaknesses or are conscious of an unhappy past, I would like to shout from the housetops, 'Find a good and lively church. Some of them at least will welcome you with open arms. Take what comes, good or ill. I have had to take words like 'backslider' and 'apostate', but I know a story that Jesus told – the story of the prodigal son. And Jesus really knew what his Father, God, was like. Go to the church and give, give, give of yourself, even if they sometimes reject you and your work. Go to the church and open your heart and trust them. You will find yourself falling into the arms of God and his forgiveness. You won't need to ask him to forgive this sin or that sin. Though do so if it helps. It's your whole being that he loves and forgives. You are his dear child and he has been longing for you. He really wants to give you the fatted calf and the beautiful new robe. Don't ever let sin and past mistakes stop you from wearing that beautiful new robe of JOY.

A factor that is a powerful antidote to sin is simple gratitude. It is seldom stressed enough in books about prayer: perhaps it is taken for granted. In casual conversations and in our private thoughts how much of our talking and thinking are devoted to complaints, grumbles, criticism. Do we give enough time to a conscious effort to think about the great mountain of blessings we enjoy and to say 'Thank you' for them? If our prayers begin with real gratitude for blessings, sin seems to slip away and to be of little importance. It is like hard ice melted by the sun of thankfulness.

The Abbé de Tourville writes,

We are all very ungrateful. If we truly believed that we are surrounded . . . with more blessings than we really need to keep up our spirits, we should be both happier and more in the Truth. We should be light hearted like those who always think they have too much, even when it seems to us they have very little indeed.[4]

This was the secret of the happiness of St Francis and the early Franciscans – their concentration on gratitude for the simplest blessings.

Neville Ward goes more deeply into the importance of this attitude of mind and the cultivation of it in prayer.[5] He shows how it can help us to cope with our fear of evil and despair. He suggests a need to develop an 'ability to delight in life, to indulge curiosity and admiration, to be interested and amused'. Unless we make 'a deliberate attempt to savour and collect the enjoyable things with which God surrounds us' we may be swamped by minor guilts and evils which can so easily pile up into serious unhappiness.

But for most old people a time comes when it is not at all easy to be grateful or to make a deliberate effort to concentrate on the happy aspects of life. When we are seriously ill or in pain, helpless and dependent on others for all we need, it is clearly difficult not to become depressed, and we perhaps find it hard to trust God. I have not had to suffer much in this way, though I have had a fair amount of caring for helpless invalids. Yet on the few occasions when I have been very weak in hospital, I find that most ordinary experiences have a new depth. Sunshine on a bright morning seems more cheerful than in normal circumstances, a bed bath and clean sheets are even more of a comfort than when one is well, the scent of some sweet peas is more intoxicating than in the sitting room at home.

Thus, in physical weakness, it is sometimes possible to concentrate pleasure on one simple thing and, perhaps, to fall into restful sleep while doing so. It is another form of thankfulness and one, to which, in old age, we might train ourselves. It is useless, when ill, to try to make prayers which put a strain

4. Abbé de Tourville, *Letters of Direction*. Amate Press (Mowbray) 1982.
5. Neville Ward, *Beyond Tomorrow*. Epworth Press 1981.

on strength. Far better to give thanks for one small blessing and to make an offering of love through it.

St Francis was able to give thanks even for Sister Death. If we are honest, it is not gratitude but fear and worry about death that command our thoughts. I have never read anything more sensible and helpful than the thoughts of the Abbé de Tourville on this subject of death:

> Do not be anxious about death . . . but give yourself up all the more to the mercy of God. No one, not even the saints can do anything else. They can only confide themselves hope-fully to God. Death is frightening only when it is far off, . . . I have seen many people die, and not one of them had the slightest fear of death, once it was there.[6]

It could be a good thing to frame a very simple prayer of trust which will admit our doubts and fears and then lean on the strength that is supporting us in the present moment. My own short prayer is, as so often, taken from a well-known hymn, 'Guide me, O Thou Great Redeemer':

> I am weak and thou art mighty
> Hold me in Thy mighty hand.

A moment of help and encouragement for some of us may be the moment of receiving the broken bread in communion, symbol of our Lord's broken body. As the priest prays that we may be preserved in eternal life so we can say 'Amen' with our hearts to that prayer.

For some people, long-term resentment for what seems an unforgivable hurt can be a serious problem. I do not associate Jesus's instruction to his disciples to forgive 'seventy times seven' (Matthew 18:22) with some incorrigible sinner, but with my own incapacity to forgive from the bottom of my heart. Moments come when I am quite sure that I have truly forgiven, and then a few days later the old resentment comes creeping back and I have to do the job over and over again – until

6. Abbé de Tourville, *Letters of Direction*.

seventy times seven. Neville Ward has some helpful advice on this matter in *Beyond Tomorrow*. He begins, 'To have something to forgive represents quite a programme.' One always hopes that the offender will acknowledge his mistake and apologize, but Neville Ward feels that this is only the superficial side of forgiveness. 'It is the release in the wounded heart that matters. When that release comes, it often changes the sufferer's attitude to the offender so that his acknowledgement and apology become secondary affairs, whether they have or have not yet occurred.' Twice, I know that I have experienced this release, and for me it comes through being for some time with the women who stayed at the foot of the cross when the men had left him.

This forgiveness is at the very heart of the Christian life, and we all need constant reminders and teaching about it. But the story of the prodigal son is both simple and profound and is all we need when we have difficulties. We need to be able to identify ourselves both with the prodigal and with the elder brother and to recognize how desperately we need the generosity of the Father whom we constantly let down and betray.

When faced with the difficulties described in this chapter, many people are able to turn to friends or to a priest for help and, of course, many lean on God's love either for relief or for a positive move towards a Christian solution. But there are problems for which there seems to be no answer. Then, often in anger, we ask ourselves the inevitable question, 'Why does God allow this to happen?' It is a question often asked in mental hospitals where some patients are no longer personalities but uncontrollable bodies with total lack of intelligence so that they can no longer feed themselves or keep themselves clean. Some exist even into old age, a burden to themselves and to others. Or there may be a lonely old man in his eighties, of subnormal intelligence all his life, brought up in institutions. In the past a tyrannical father and a criminal, he is now, in old age, deserted by children and grandchildren, an isolated heap of bitterness, living in dirt and afflicted with constant ill health.

There are thousands of deprived people who feel they have 'never had a chance' and spend all their lives in an atmosphere of squalor, hard words, ugly environment, bitterness and anger until their death.

There are others who are embittered because they look back to opportunities missed or opportunities that never came their way. 'Sour old maid' is a phrase that I have heard many times in my life to describe an elderly single woman, shut in on her own misery, a prey to her hidden unsatisfied longing for husband and children.

Readers of this book will almost all know something of the things that are 'lovely and of good report', of friendship and kindness, of gardens or books or music, of delight in family relationships. But there are many who know nothing of our joy, of our defences against evil, our reliefs from monotony and loneliness. I can see no clear answer, just a suggestion perhaps in the parable of the good Samaritan (Luke 10:30–5). In the old prayer book service there is a sentence about the good Samaritan: 'He came to where he was.' That is, the good Samaritan crossed right over the road to the Jew who had been battered and deserted. When we find people who are stripped naked by the circumstances in their life, who have nothing left to make it bearable, we may feel helpless. There is perhaps one simple thing we can do. We can take the sufferer's hand and, through our grasp, pour all the love and longing to understand of which we are capable. It must say something even though there seems to be no response. The healing power of Jesus will surely flow in some measure through our hand though no words may ever be spoken. There is an ancient prayer that might meet our own need when we feel overcome by the forces of evil and which we could pray on behalf of those who do not know how to pray for themselves. It is called the '*Anima Christi*' or 'The Soul of Christ'.

Jesus, may all that is you flow into me,
May your body and blood be my food and drink.
May your passion and death be my strength and life,

Jesus, with you by my side enough has been given,
May the shelter I seek be the shadow of your cross,
Let me not run from the love which you offer,
But hold me safe from the forces of evil.
On each of my dyings shed your light and your love,
Keep calling to me until that day comes,
When with your saints, I may praise you for ever.
Amen.

For those who have worries or doubts about death a prayer by
Henry Scott Holland may offer reassurance.

Death is nothing at all, I have only slipped away into the
next room.
I am I and you are you, whatever we were to each other we
are still.
Call me by my old familiar name, speak to me in the easy
way which we always used.
Put no difference into your tone; wear no forced air of
solemnity or sorrow.
Laugh as we always laughed at the little jokes together.
Pray, smile, think of me, pray for me.
. . .
What is this death but a negligible accident? Why should I
be out of mind because I am out of sight? I am but waiting
for you, for an interval, somewhere very near, just around
the corner.
All is well.

6

The Banquet

In one of his well known poems, George Herbert describes prayer as the 'Church's banquet'.[1] It is a true and lovely description. I suppose all of us have been, on several occasions, to extravagant parties with delicious food, and most of us may well have provided a banquet to celebrate a wedding or a twenty-first birthday or some special moment of success or happiness. The generous provision of good food and drink are the basics for a banquet, and anyone who says that he is not interested in these things seems to me to be rejecting some of God's happiest gifts to us all. But all kinds of other things play a part, the appearance and decoration of the dining room or hall, the company and their talk, their clothes, manners and kindness, perhaps music, dancing, speeches.

Without any doubt the prayer offered to me in the last five years by the Church has been a spiritual banquet. It has been a great feast of spiritual food, generous, nourishing, energizing and interesting because of the different environments in which it is made and the great variety of people who offer prayer in so many different ways. My own private prayer can be similarly rich and varied, provided I make some small effort to help myself to the good things offered by God. The banquet offered in prayer is not just there for rare occasions. It can be ours at all times if we choose, though naturally we often concentrate on one 'dish' or kind of prayer according to our need of the moment. But I am always fully aware of all the other wonderful

1. From 'Prayer' in George Herbert's *Poems*. World's Classics (O.U.P.).

dishes waiting for me at the Lord's banquet and that I am free to help myself to them when I need or choose.

Usually the happiest gift of any party for me is the offering of friendship and relationship. We meet people with whom we have family ties, or ties of affection or of business interests. We usually put on our good clothes and turn our best selves outwards for these occasions. There is an hour or two in which to grow into a deeper and finer and more trusting relationship. So it is in the banquet of prayer. The quiet growth of friendship, of trusting relationship has been a rich offering from my Lord who bids me welcome to his banquet. When my thoughts are ugly or resentful, I do not need to pretend by putting on a pretty spiritual manner in prayer, yet it is an act of good manners to admit the unclean things and to try to get rid of them, as in a bath, and to try to offer my Lord a nosegay of gratitude or an act of adoration or a humble entreaty for his presence and help.

Before I became a part of the Church, people and their friendship, their interesting diversity, their gifts, affection, oddities seemed the best thing in my life. Now it is even more so. Although one Friend has become all in all there is a paradox. Because he is all in all, the others matter far more than they did before I knew him. One learns to love them in a newer, simpler way. The old criticisms, comparisons, suspicions, jealousies, envies gradually slip away because there is no place for these foolish things in the friendship offered by my Lord at his banquet. The love I take from my friends and try to give to them slowly becomes steadier and stronger without mistrust and complications. But it is a very slow and quiet process. In one or two cases a really bad relationship of dislike has been changed into one of affection. Sometimes it happens with very little effort. I am reminded of a verse from a hymn often sung in childhood, 'Souls of men, why will ye scatter' – a bit sentimental perhaps, but summing up the cheerful uncomplicated nature of the new relationship.

> If our love were but more simple
> We should take Him at His word,
> And our lives would be all sunshine,
> In the sweetness of the Lord.

Of course this happiness in relationship is a nourishing and appetizing dish offered in the banquet of prayer. There is another with a similar nature and that is forgiveness. Already much has been said about this in earlier chapters but I suggest the Abbé de Tourville sums up how gladly we should receive it.

> Accept everything from Him, however ungrateful, however 'unrepaying' you may be. Receive again and again. Rejoice in receiving without afterthought. . . . Think always of that which you receive, never of that which you give. This is a far better way of entering into the love of our Lord and acquiring a boundless confidence in Him, than by looking at yourself and thinking of what you can do for Him.[2]

There may be a few readers who feel their past neglect is so great that forgiveness is out of the question. They cannot forgive themselves. Yet another poem by George Herbert gives the perfect answer to such diffidence. Quite certainly there is no long-term indifference which God will not forgive provided we turn to him at last. In this poem God pleads with us to forgive ourselves. The poem has the simple title 'Love'.[3]

> Love bade me welcome; yet my soul drew back,
>   Guilty of dust and sin.
> But quick-eyed Love, observing me grow slack
>   From my first entrance in,
> Drew nearer to me, sweetly questioning
>   If I lack'd anything.

2. Abbé de Tourville, *Letters of Direction*.
3. George Herbert, *Poems*. World's Classics (O.U.P.).

'A guest,' I answer'd, 'worthy to be here';
    Love said, 'You shall be he.'
'I, the unkind, ungrateful? Ah, my dear,
    I cannot look on Thee.'
Love took my hand, and smiling did reply,
    'Who made the eyes but I?'

'Truth, Lord; but I have marr'd them; let my shame
    Go where it doth deserve.'
'And know you not,' says Love, 'Who bore the blame?'
    'My dear, then I will serve.'
'You must sit down,' says Love, 'and taste my meat.'
    So I did sit and eat.

Perhaps that poem is the most perfect expression we have in our language of the relationship between God and a penitent human being half afraid to approach him and yet longing to know him and to love him. So many of us have been in that case at some time or another.

At any banquet we are usually offered some sharp sauces to accompany rich dishes. Caper sauce or mint sauce is served with rich roast lamb, apple sauce with pork, horseradish with beef. There is a parallel in the spiritual banquet. Even in old age there are experiences which can sometimes be bitter to taste and yet they give relish to the richer dishes of friendship and forgiveness just described. One of the sharp spiritual sauces of old age is vulnerability. We do get hurt in old age just because we are old. We can no longer live our physical lives with the zest of twenty years past and, because of it, we often feel that we are on the shelf. Children and grandchildren may be very kind and visit us occasionally but there will be other times when they are so busy with their own affairs that they forget us and we are hurt. We try to say firmly to ourselves, 'They have their own lives to lead.' But they are moving into greater fullness of life while we are receding into inactivity. They are accepting new responsibilities; we are surrendering ours. We can easily become despondent.

We may even wish to be reconciled with an old enemy, to

soften the memory of past hurts given or received. If we pluck up our courage and hold out the hand of friendship, it can at times be cruelly slapped back. There may be a handful of old people or of saints who do not have these experiences or feelings, but I suspect that most old people know this sharp sauce of hurt and vulnerability. It is a part of the banquet, for it gives us an opportunity to share the hurt with our Lord and in his strength to accept it. We may even, with his help, begin to laugh at the hurts of old age and, in so doing, realize the comic side of our inadequacies. So, in humility, a new self can be born, a self that may surprise us as fun and delight bubble up at unexpected moments and there will be a deeper kindness both for others and for ourselves. But it won't always be fun. Vulnerability can mean pain and moments of lonely anguish. When they come, it could be wise to take the advice of an old Yorkshire minister I once knew whose concluding words to a farewell sermon were, 'Gie a hand to Jesus and stick.'

It works. Because nothing matters so much as to try to stay close to our Lord and to try to pray with complete honesty. He was hurt so much more than any of us because he loved infinitely more. Perhaps prayers and tears and the new kind of loving vulnerability will all struggle together in confusion. Yet out of the confusion we can turn to him and lean on his strength. In the recognition of his suffering and the acceptance of our own we shall find the gift of his peace.

We shall not only find the gift of his peace but we shall find him everywhere and we shall find a new kind of spiritual life in old age. It has just happened that it is with place rather than with time that my prayers are usually associated. At any moment of the day I can know the presence of my Lord in my untidy little sitting room where I am typing at the moment. I can share with him everything I am doing, unless I am in a very rebellious mood. On a road into town, with heavy traffic always flowing, I can give him thanks and praise and sing 'Alleluia' out loud. On Sunday, in our lovely, quiet churchyard, I can pray with all the saints who have given, and are giving, so much to St Peter's. In bed, I can say two or three words in rhythm as I drop off to sleep, like 'Abba, Father,' or 'The grace of our Lord Jesus Christ'. It may be a healthful, physical practice for I notice that my breathing grows slower and more rhythmical, and I drop off to sleep more easily.

To return to the early pages of this book and to Fred Milson's article 'Face to Faith':

> We are not prisoners of the passing years, psychological and physical determinism does not tell the whole story. Bones which feel the east wind more keenly, a failing memory whose filing clerk has become arthritic, are undeniable realities. But, so too, is the Spirit of God, whereby our youth can be renewed like the eagle's.

There are so many other dishes in this banquet – strength that can carry any burden, holy wisdom to meet any perplexity, joy that dispels fear and depression, humility to meet us at our own level and scatter foolish pride. It would take a separate book to write about them all.

But there is one offering at the banquet of which I have recently become more aware. A few months ago, I was in Assisi, the town where St Francis worked and to which he returned after strenuous preaching tours. Immediately after his conversion, he spoke of a new love that had been born in him for God's creatures. He said that he had never really seen the sky, the rocks, the sun and moon, the flowers, the streams, as he saw them when he had stripped himself of all his possessions, even his clothes, and 'embraced' Lady Poverty. He found his 'Most High Lord' in all these lovely gifts that are given to all of us in lavish abundance. In the strength of a driving wind, in the great billowing white clouds that race across the unbelievable blue of an Italian sky, in the flowers that grow in the cracks of the walls, in the poppies among the wheat, in the grapes ripening in midday heat, in the refreshing water of a wayside spring, in the tall dignity of the poplars, in the life of the rabbits and mice, the lizards and the crickets that lived and multiplied all round the poor little church of San Damiano, he accepted a banquet of love from God. His eyes were opened to know them as God's creatures and to make them a part of his worship and adoration. It can happen to us, and not only in Italy, if we open our eyes to see and our hearts to love. I find that I am even looking at spiders and earwigs and worms with new eyes.

This last paragraph was written yesterday on the eve of St Francis day, which is 4 October. The manuscript had been pushed aside for two or three months because I had many other things to do, and to conclude a book is always the hardest thing for a novice writer. I could not find a way to do it. This morning we had a lovely Eucharist in our church followed by a merry St Francis breakfast. Then I came home and said to myself, 'Forget everything: leave the chores. Sit down and read the book straight through and then try to sum up its truth – its truth for you – and don't try to be clever.' At the end I did what St Francis did when he was in despair. I put my head down on my arms and howled my eyes out. Through the tears I spoke the truth, 'Dear Lord, I'm a bloody hypocrite.' It seemed a hopeless end to an adventure started so confidently with Abraham on page 1. But, of course, it is not the end but just one more beginning. Those of you who are septuagenarians or older will know what tears can do and what truth can do, too. They clear away the mists. They give us a blessing of gentleness and help us to move one step nearer to God's enfolding love. That I have written of many things which I know and live very imperfectly is not of serious consequence to God's purposes. He will take care of it. A preacher in the pulpit has to do this. It is God's truth he tries to preach, not his own, and it is God's will that he should preach with zeal and love. So I ask the forgiveness of my readers in writing of many things of which I still have so much to learn.

But many of my elderly readers will share one experience with me. We have been through two wars. We long for peace for our children and for our children's children. Perhaps we could go back to the start of this book where we tried to say a short prayer very frequently. The first two lines of the prayer ascribed to St Francis hold a truth for all of us who long for peace. We could say it regularly, with all the loving thought of which we are capable. Prayer is never lost even if wars come.

> Lord, make me an instrument of your peace.
> Where there is hatred, let me sow love.
>
> . . .
>
> Let me sow love.

Suggestions for Further Reading

The books listed here are ones which the writer has found helpful (several of them are referred to in chapter 3). Many of these books can be obtained from bookshops selling religious literature or from church bookstalls. It may be possible to borrow some from diocesan libraries.

GEORGE APPLETON
Praying with the Bible. Bible Reading Fellowship, 1981.

ANTHONY BLOOM
School for Prayer. Darton Longman and Todd, 1970.
(jointly with Georges Lefebvre, O.S.B.), *Courage to Pray*. Darton Longman and Todd, 1973.

CHRISTOPHER BRYANT
The River Within. Darton Longman and Todd, 1978.
The Heart in Pilgrimage: Christian Guidelines for the Human Journey. Darton Longman and Todd, 1980.

CARLO CARRETTO
I, Francis: Spirit of St Francis of Assisi. Fount (Collins), 1982.

SHEILA CASSIDY
Audacity to Believe. Fount (Collins), 1978.
Prayer for Pilgrims. Fount (Collins), 1980.

RICHARD HOLLOWAY
The Killing. Darton Longman and Todd, 1984.

JULIAN OF NORWICH
Revelations of Divine Love (translated by C. Wolters). Penguin, 1973.
Enfolded in Love (extracts from the *Revelations* selected and translated by members of the Julian Shrine). Darton Longman and Todd, 1980.

ST TERESA OF AVILA
The Interior Castle (translated by Kieran Kavanaugh, O.C.D., and Otilio Rodriguez, O.C.D.). S.P.C.K., 1979.

FRANK TOPPING
Lord of the Morning. Lutterworth Press, 1977.
Lord of the Evening. Lutterworth Press, 1979.

ABBÉ DE TOURVILLE
Letters of Direction. Amate Press (Mowbray), 1982.

W. H. VANSTONE
Love's Endeavour, Love's Expense. Darton Longman and Todd, 1977.

ESTHER DE WAAL
Seeking God. Fount (Collins), 1984.

NEVILLE WARD
Five for Sorrow, Ten for Joy. Epworth Press, 1971.
Friday Afternoon. Epworth Press, 1976.
Beyond Tomorrow. Epworth Press, 1981.

HARRY WILLIAMS
Becoming What I Am. Darton Longman and Todd, 1977.
God's Wisdom in Christ's Cross. Mirfield Publications, 1978.
True Resurrection. Fount (Collins), 1983.